Old Testament Geography

By
Matt Hennecke and Philip Chumbley

Truth
Publications

*Taking His hand,
helping each other home.*
™

ISBN 10: 1-58427-175-2

ISBN 13: 978-1-58427-175-8

First Printing: 2006

Truth Publications, Inc.
CEI Bookstore
220 S. Marion St., Athens, AL 35611
855-492-6657
sales@truthpublications.com
www.truthbooks.com

CONTENTS

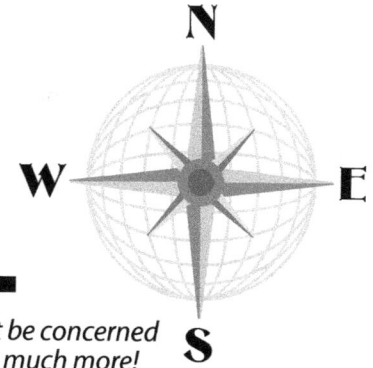

NOTE: *You may find it easier to answer the following questions if you use a modern atlas and the maps in the back of your Bible. Don't be concerned if you cannot answer all the questions as this exercise is designed to see what you already know. By the end of this study you will know much more!*

1. If you were to visit the site of the ancient city of Babylon, in what modern country would you be?
   A. Israel   B. Arabia   C. Turkey   D. Iran   E. Iraq

2. If you were to visit the ancient city of Damascus, in what modern country would you be (Isa. 7:8)?
   A. Turkey   B. Lebanon   C. Syria   D. Jordan   E. Egypt

3. If you were to visit the ancient city of Ur, in what modern country would you be?
   A. Israel   B. Arabia   C. Turkey   D. Iran   E. Iraq

4. If you were to visit the ancient city of Jerusalem, in what modern country would you be?
   A. Israel   B. Arabia   C. Turkey   D. Iran   E. Iraq

5. About how high is the highest mountain in the region of Canaan? (See page 8 for help in answering this question.)
   A. About 10,000 feet
   B. About 5,000 feet
   C. About 2,500 feet
   D. About 1,000 feet
   E. About 500 feet

6. What is the highest mountain in the region of Canaan (Josh. 12:1)?
   A. Nebo   B. Horeb   C. Hermon   D. Carmel   E. Zion

7. What major caravan route ran north and south through Canaan just east of the Jordan River (Num. 20:17; 21:22)?
   A. The Way of the Plain
   B. The Way of Egypt
   C. The Way of the Sea
   D. The Via Maris
   E. The King's Highway

8. What is the approximate distance between where the Jordan River exits the Sea of Galilee to where it joins the Salt Sea? (See page 7 for help in answering this question.)
   A. About 210 miles
   B. About 170 miles
   C. About 110 miles
   D. About 70 miles
   E. About 30 miles

9. What is the approximate elevation of the city of Jerusalem? (See page 8w for help in answering this question.)
   A. About 3,600 feet
   B. About 2,600 feet
   C. About 1,600 feet
   D. About 600 feet
   E. About sea level

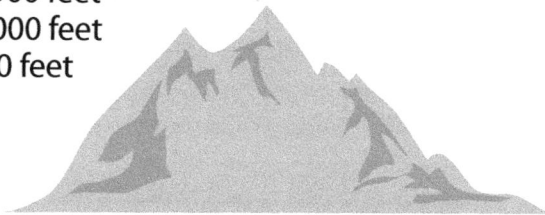

© 2020 Truth Publications, Inc.

THE MIDDLE EAST – Review Map #1

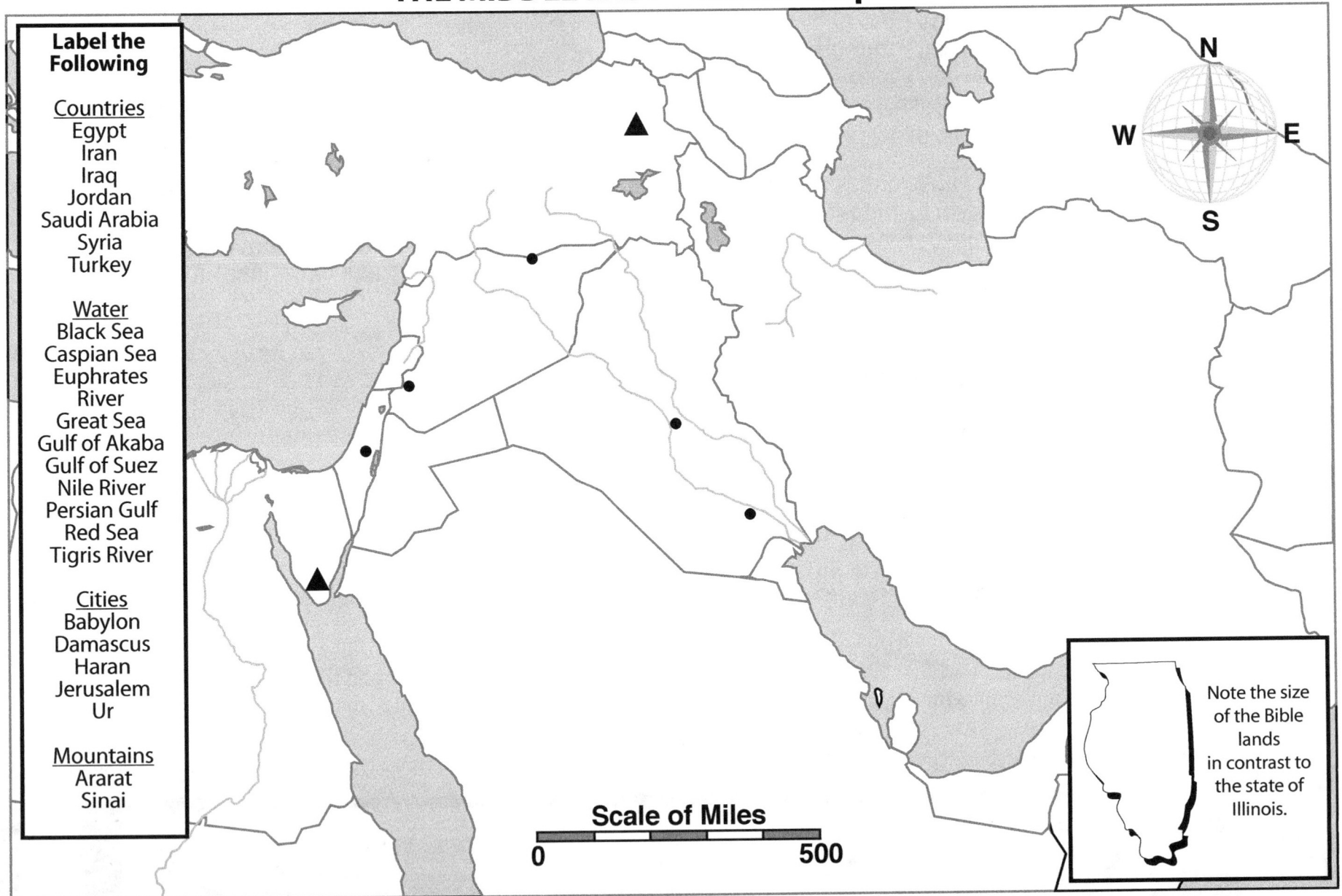

Label the Following

Countries
Egypt
Iran
Iraq
Jordan
Saudi Arabia
Syria
Turkey

Water
Black Sea
Caspian Sea
Euphrates River
Great Sea
Gulf of Akaba
Gulf of Suez
Nile River
Persian Gulf
Red Sea
Tigris River

Cities
Babylon
Damascus
Haran
Jerusalem
Ur

Mountains
Ararat
Sinai

N
W   E
S

Scale of Miles
0   500

Note the size of the Bible lands in contrast to the state of Illinois.

NOTE: *You will find it easier to label this map and the one on the next page if you use a modern atlas and the maps in the back of your Bible. If you can't fully complete the two maps, do the best you can. By the conclusion of this study you will be able to complete these maps with no difficulty.*

Label the Following

Countries
Egypt
Israel
Jordan
Lebanon
Saudi Arabia
Syria

Water
Arnon River
Dead Sea
Great Sea
Jordan River
Jabbok River
Sea of Galilee
Yarmuk River
Zered River

Cities
Damascus
Jerusalem

Mountains
Carmel
Ebal
Gerizim
Hermon
Nebo

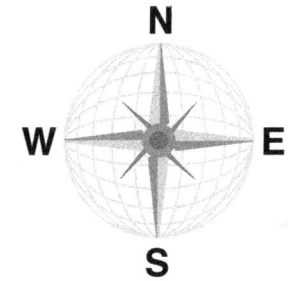

From the southern end of the Sea of Galilee to the northern end of the Dead Sea is about 68 miles.

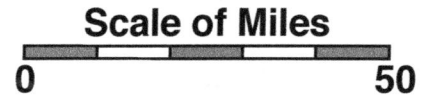

N
W   E
S

Scale of Miles
0   50

CROSS SECTION OF CANAAN

© 1999 MANNA

Cross Section (South to North)

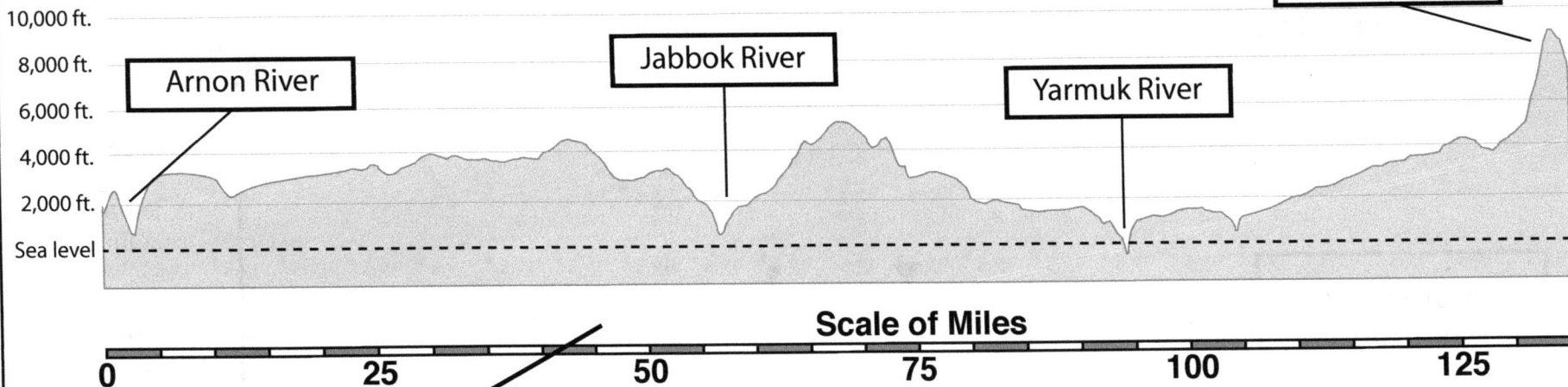

Mount Hermon

Arnon River

Jabbok River

Yarmuk River

10,000 ft.
8,000 ft.
6,000 ft.
4,000 ft.
2,000 ft.
Sea level

Scale of Miles

0   25   50   75   100   125

Cross Section (West to East)

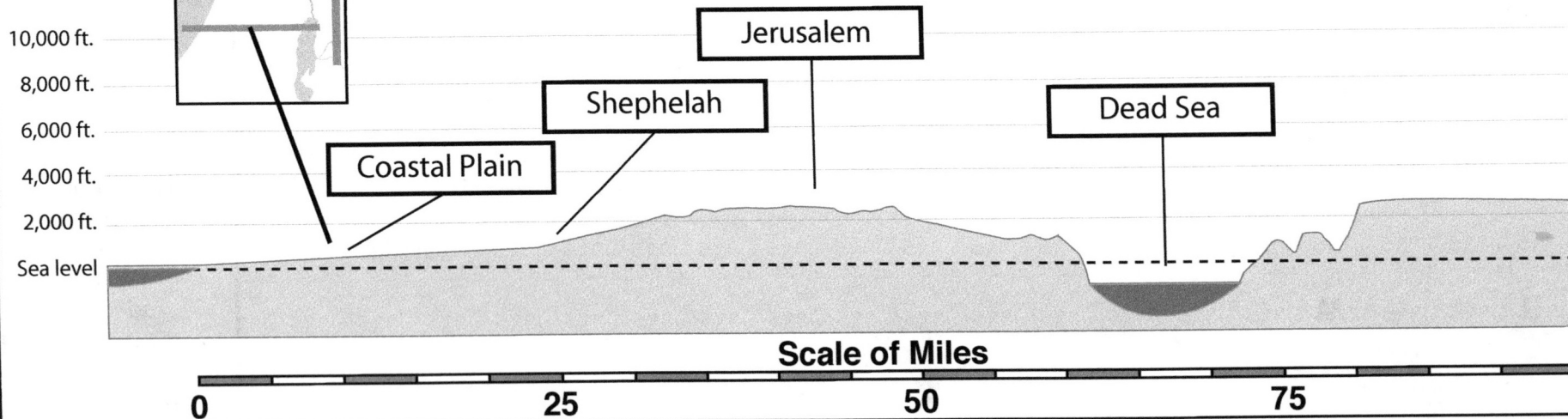

Jerusalem

Shephelah

Dead Sea

Coastal Plain

10,000 ft.
8,000 ft.
6,000 ft.
4,000 ft.
2,000 ft.
Sea level

Scale of Miles

0   25   50   75

OLD TESTAMENT GEOGRAPHY
Beginnings

Abram was called by God.

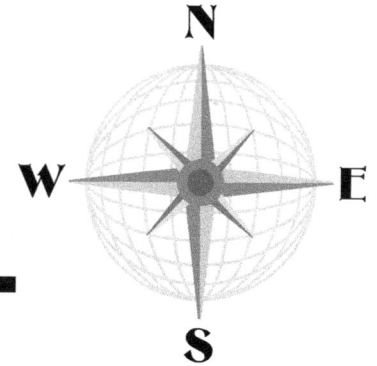

1. What four rivers mentioned specifically in the Bible give us an idea of the location of the Garden of Eden (Gen. 2:10-14)?

   _____   _____

   _____   _____

2. In what modern country might the site of the ancient Garden of Eden lie? (Hint: Bagdad is the capital of this country.)
   A. Kuwait   B. Arabia   C. Turkey   D. Iran   E. Iraq

3. Where according to the Bible was the Tower of Babel built (Gen. 11:2-9)?
   A. Babylon   B. Shinar   C. Mespotamia   D. Canaan   E. Egypt

4. Where was Abram when he received a call from God to go to a land that He would show him (Gen. 11:31-32; 12:1)?
   A. Haran   B. Shechem   C. Babylon   D. Ur   E. Mari

5. How far westward did Abraham travel before finally settling in Canaan (Gen.12:10)?
   A. Egypt   B. Negev   C. Ashdod   D. Tyre   E. Haran

6. What two *major* rivers dominate the region that came to be known as the Fertile Crescent?
   A. Tigris   B. Diala   C. Zab   D. Euphrates   E. Habor

7. Why do you think the "Fertile Crescent" is so named?

   _____

8. Near what river was the ancient city of Ur? (See page 11.)
   A. Habor   B. Tigris   C. Euphrates   D. Diala   E. Zab

9. In what city did Abram's wife Sarah die? (Gen.23:2)
   A. Haran   B. Ur   C. Kirjath-arba   D. Hebron   E. Bethel

10. It is thought by some that the ancient cities of Sodom and Gomorrah are buried under what body of water? (See Jer. 49:17-18 and the map on page 18.)
    A. Dead Sea   B. Sea of Galilee   C. Great Sea   D. Hula Lake

11. On or near what mount was Abraham told to sacrifice Isaac (Gen. 22:2)?
    A. Moriah   B. Hebron   C. Nebo   D. Sinai   E. Carmel

12. What was later built on or near the mount upon which Abraham was told to sacrifice Isaac (2 Chron. 3:1)?
    A. An altar   B. A shrine   C. A temple   D. A tower   E. A city

13. When he died, where was Abraham buried? Who else was buried there according to the Bible (Gen. 23:19; 25:9; 49:31; 50:13-14)?

    _____

    _____

BEGINNINGS

Label the Following

Features
Garden of Eden
Mt. Ararat
Shinar
Fertile Crescent
Cave of Machpelah
Negev

Water
Dead Sea
Tigris River
Euphrates River
Persian Gulf

Cities
Ur
Haran
Mari
Shechem
Damascus
Bethel
Kirjath-arba
Sodom & Gomorrah
Beer-sheba
Salem

Scale of Miles
0   200

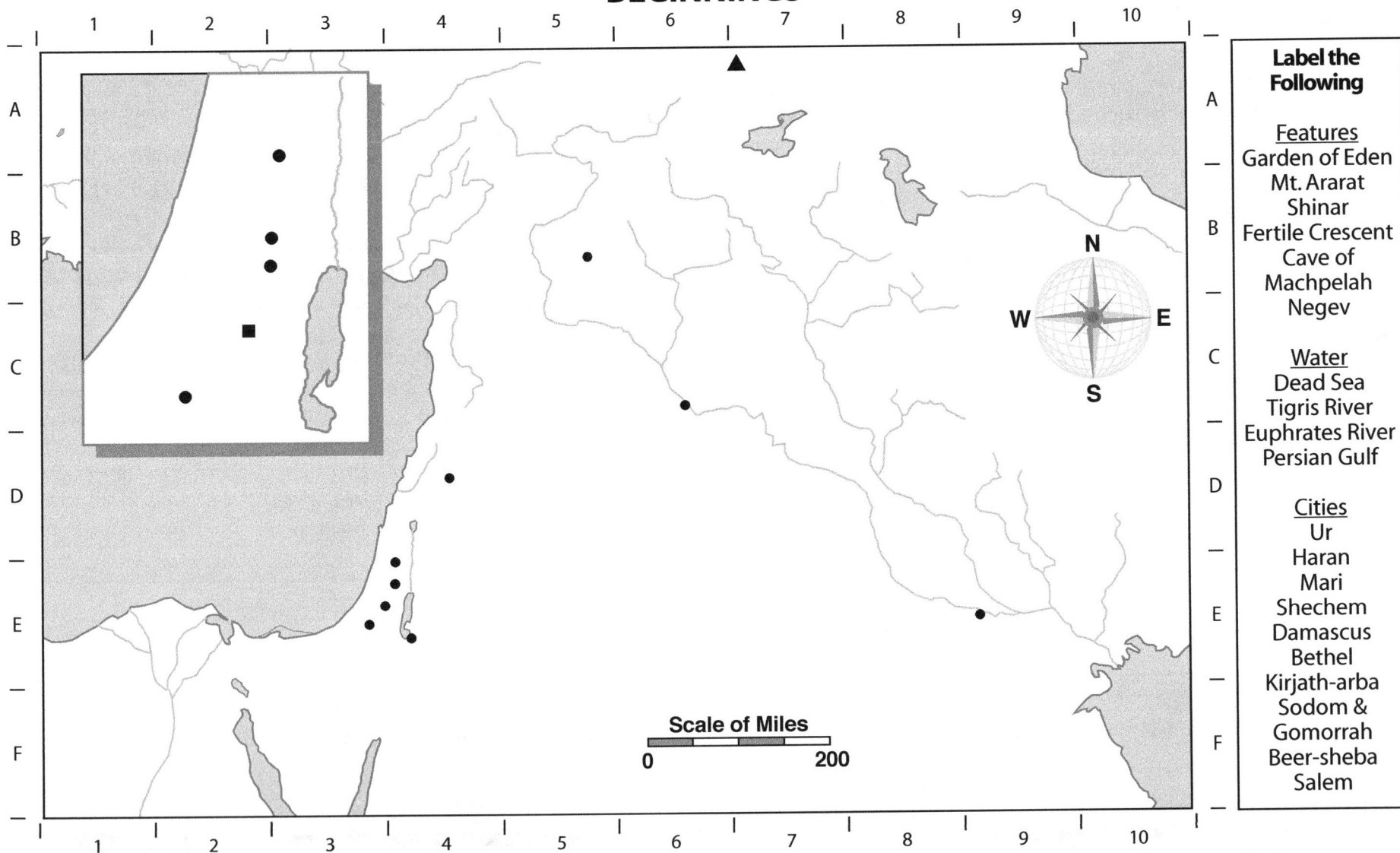

READ THE FOLLOWING Indicate locations by putting the appropriate letter/number intersection. (Example: E9 is the location of Ur.)

√ **The Garden of Eden** – Genesis 2:10-15 • Where is it thought the Garden of Eden was located? _____

√ **The Flood and the Mountains of Ararat** – Genesis 8:1-4 • Where are the mountains of Ararat? _____

√ **The Tower of Babel and Dispersion of People** – Genesis 11:1-9 • Where was the Tower of Babel? _____

√ **The Promise and Journey of Abraham** – Genesis 11:27-32; 12:1-10; 13:1-18; 15:7; 18-21; 22:1-2; 23:1-2; 25:8-11 • Trace the journey of Abraham.

ANCIENT CITY OF UR

Ur of the Chaldees

The population of Ur is estimated to have been

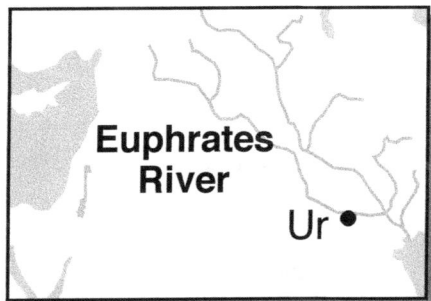

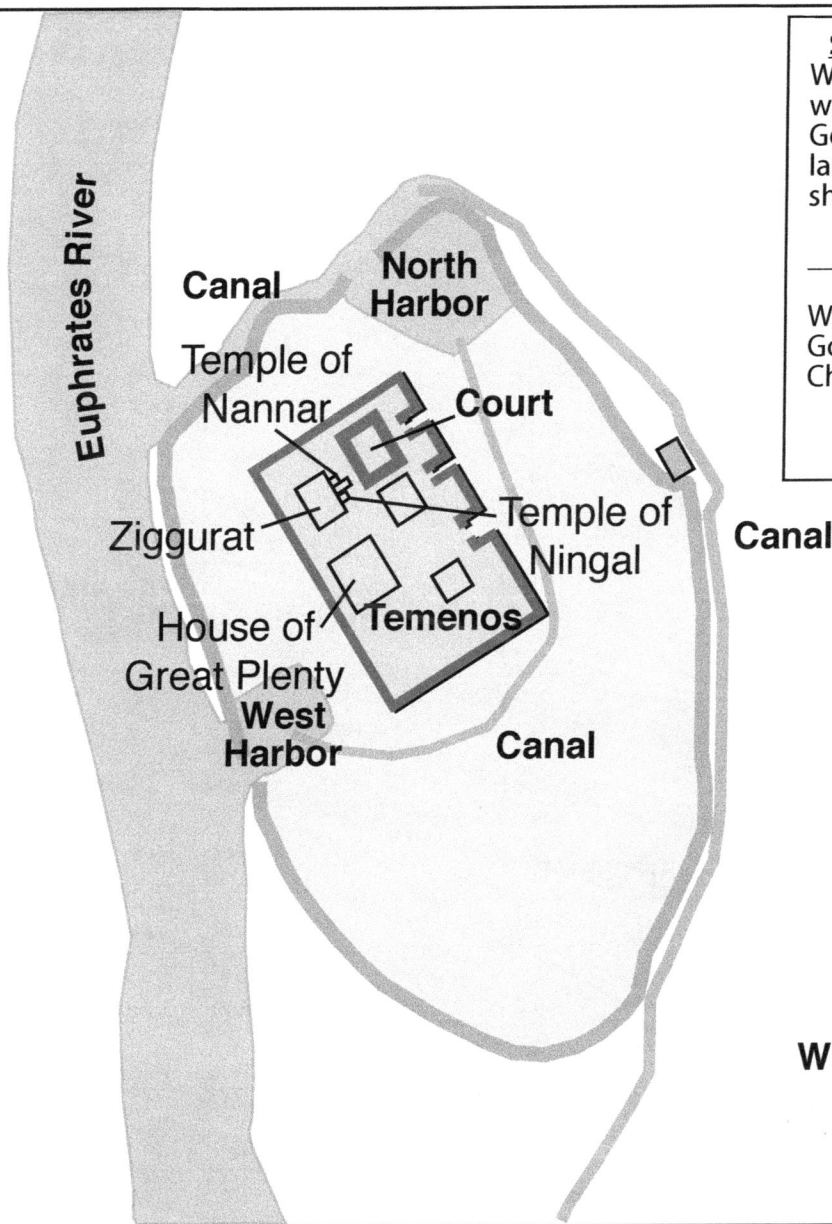

_____

Euphrates River

Ur •

Scale of Feet

0   2000

Euphrates River

Canal

North Harbor

Temple of Nannar

Court

Ziggurat

Temple of Ningal

Canal

House of Great Plenty

Temenos

West Harbor

Canal

N
W   E
S

SOME QUESTIONS
Where was Abraham when he was *called* by God in Genesis 12 to a land that God would show him (Gen. 11:31)?

_____

Was Abraham called by God to leave Ur of the Chaldees (see Neh. 9:7)?

___ Yes ___ No

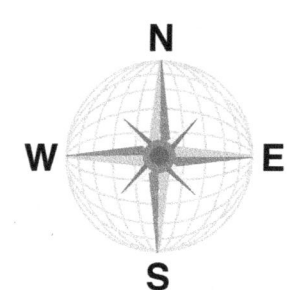

MOUNT MORIAH AND THE TEMPLE

QUESTIONS FOR DISCUSSION

Did Abraham nearly sacrifice Isaac at the site of the future temple? Read the following then be ready to defend your answer.

1. Where was Abraham at the time of the command to sacrifice Isaac (Gen. 21:34)?

2. How long did it take for Abraham and Isaac travel to the site (Gen. 22:4)?

3. Is any reference made to Abraham when the site of the temple is mentioned (2 Chron. 3:1)?

Bethesda Valley

Outline of present temple Mount in Jerusalem

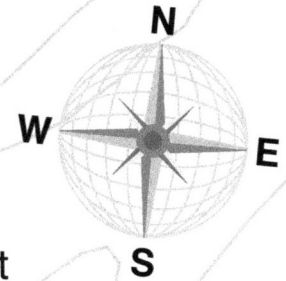

N
W   E
S

+ **Mt. Moriah**

Tyropoeon Valley

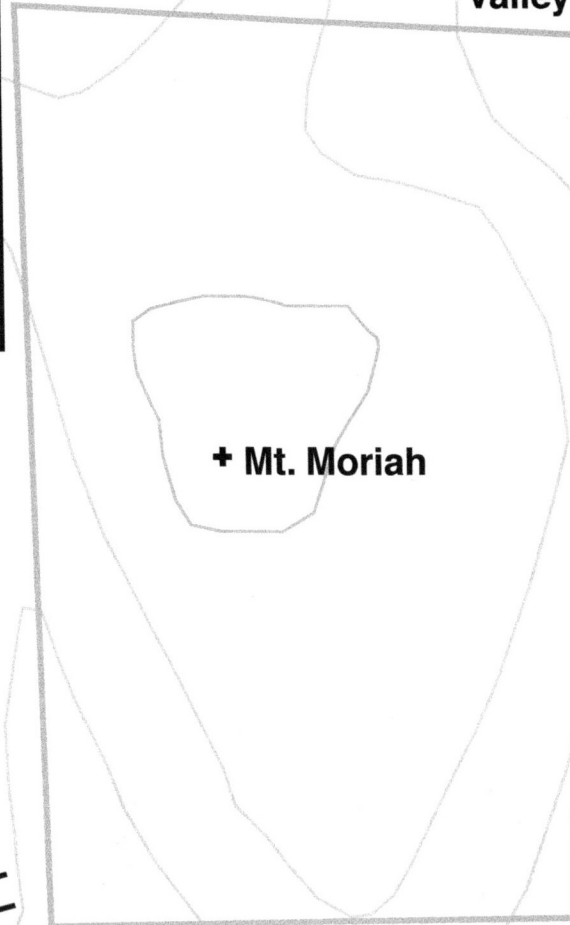

Kidron Valley

Olivet

Scale of Feet

0   500

3 OLD TESTAMENT GEOGRAPHY
Egypt, the Exodus, and 40 Year Wandering

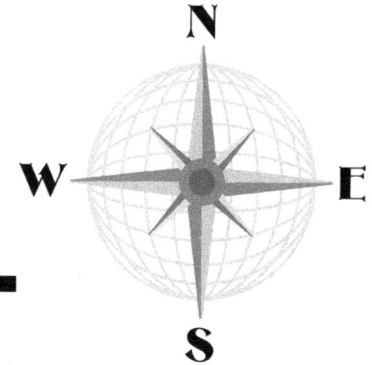

1. How did God's people end up in Egypt? Why do you think they were sent into Egypt by God? (See Gen. 15:13-14.)

_____

_____

_____

_____

2. While in Egypt, where did God's people settle (Gen. 47:27)?
A. Mizraim   B. Goshen   C. Delta   D. Shur   E. Paran

3. What two treasure (storage) cities did the Israelites build while in servitude in Egypt? (Exo. 1:11)
A. Rameses   B. Pithom   C. Tanis   D. Memphis   E. Succoth

4. Into what land did Moses flee after killing an Egyptian (Exo. 2:15)?
A. Moab   B. Ammon   C. Zin   D. Midian   E. Canaan

5. Where did the Amalekites first attack God's people (Exo. 17:8)?
A. Rephidim   B. Elim   C. Succoth   D. Hormah   E. Oboth

6. Where is Mount Sinai located (See Exo. 3:1; 32:1-4; Psa. 106:19.)?
A. Land of Midian   B. Sinai Peninsula   C. Canaan   D. Edom

7. In what mountain did Moses receive the 10 commandments (Exo. 34:1-4)?
A. Hor   B. Horeb   C. Sinai   D. Nebo   E. Zion

8. From what wilderness did Moses send spies to spy out the land of Canaan (Num. 13:21)?
A. Paran   B. Zin   C. Shur   D. Etham   E. Sin

9. How many days did the spies spy out the land of Canaan (Num. 13:25)?
A. 10   B. 20   C. 30   D. 40   E. 50

10. About how far north would you guess the spies travelled in searching out the land?
A. 50 miles   B. 100 miles   C. 150 miles   D. 200 miles

11. In what mountain did Aaron die (Num. 33:38)?
A. Hor   B. Nebo   C. Sinai   D. Zion   E. Horeb

THE EXODUS – Traditional Route

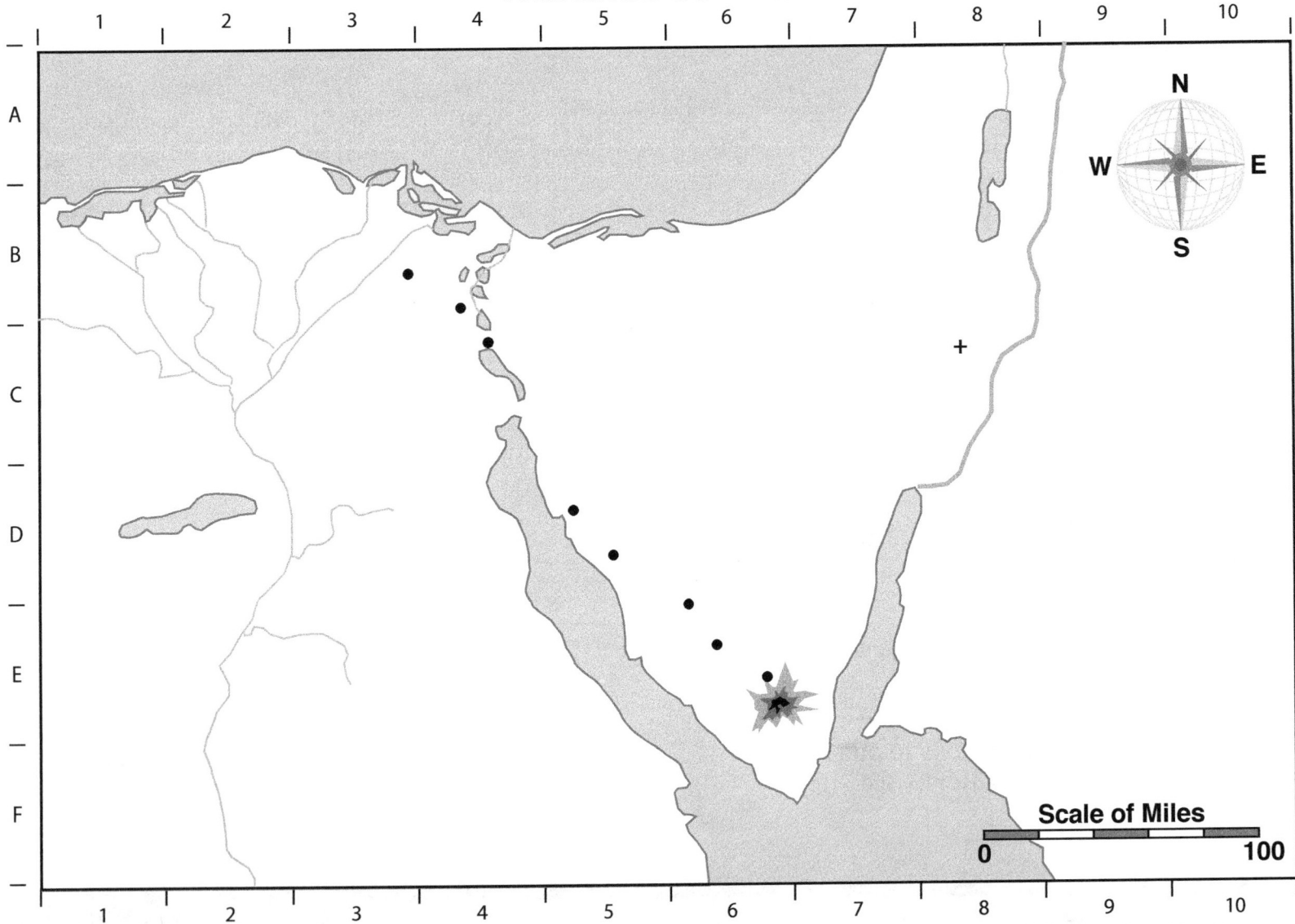

Label the Following

Features
Nile Delta
Mount Sinai
Egypt
Goshen
Sinai Peninsula
Land of Midian
Mt. Hor*
King's Highway

Water
Red Sea
Gulf of Suez
Gulf of Akaba
Great Sea
Dead Sea
Jordan River
Bitter Lakes
Nile River

Locations
Rameses
Etham
Marah
Elim
Dophkah
Alush
Rephidim

READ THE FOLLOWING: Indicate locations by putting the letter/number intersection. (Example: A8 is the Dead Sea.)

√ **How God's People Came to be in Egypt** – Genesis 26:1-3; 37:28; 46:3-4; 47:6 • Where is the land of Goshen? _____

√ **Moses Flees** – Exodus 2:11-21; 3:1-10 • Where was the land of Midian? _____ Where is Mount Sinai (Horeb)? _____

√ **The Exodus** – Exodus 12:37-39; 14:5-31 • Trace the journey of the Exodus to Mt. Sinai.

Be ready to discuss the location of Mt. Sinai. What alternative location is suggested by Exodus 2:15-21?

*The exact location is unknown.

THE TABERNACLE

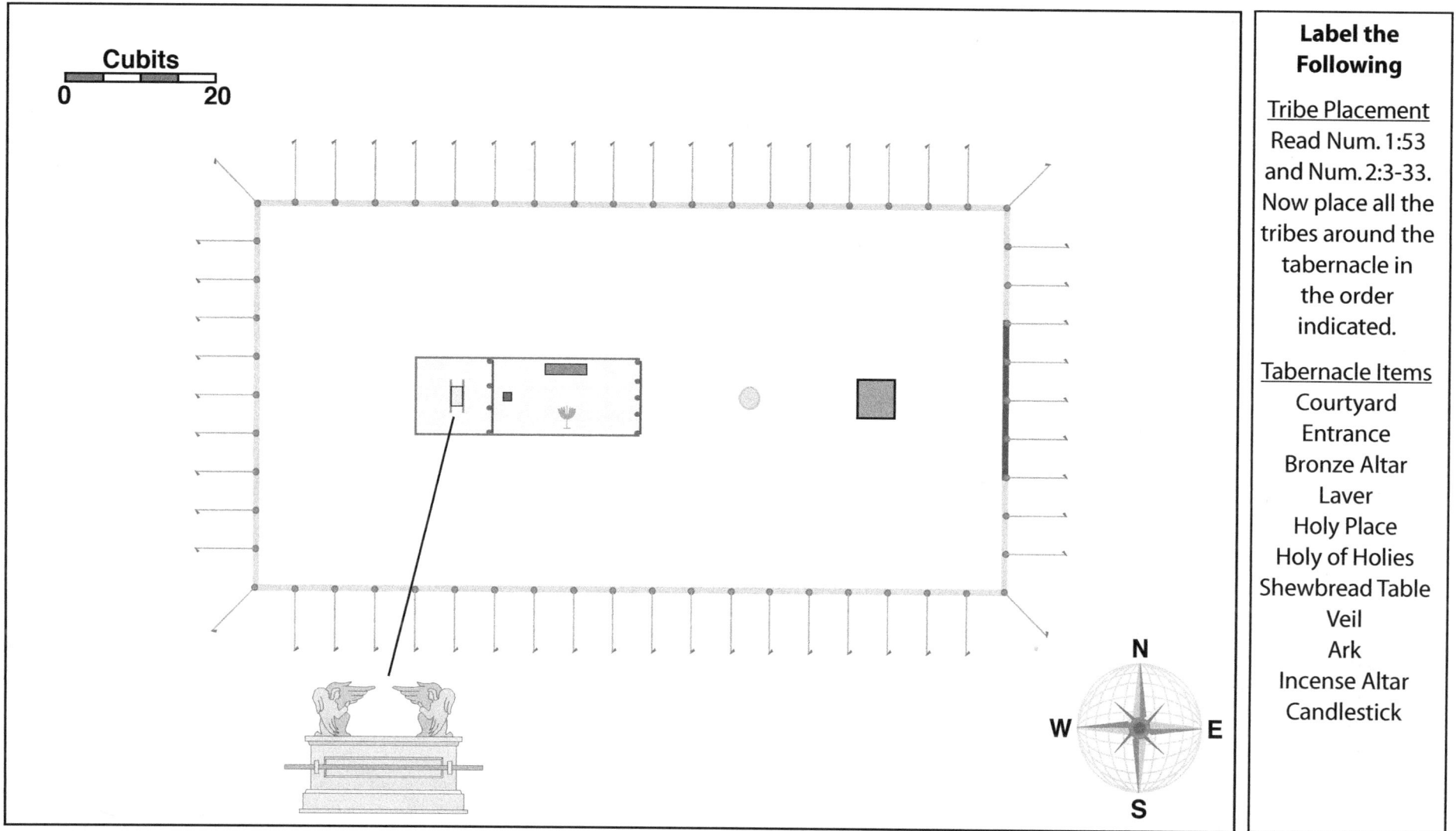

Cubits
0   20

Label the Following

Tribe Placement
Read Num. 1:53 and Num. 2:3-33. Now place all the tribes around the tabernacle in the order indicated.

Tabernacle Items
Courtyard
Entrance
Bronze Altar
Laver
Holy Place
Holy of Holies
Shewbread Table
Veil
Ark
Incense Altar
Candlestick

N
W   E
S

TABERNCLE: From the Hebrew word *mishkan* which literally means "residence" or "dwelling," the tabernacle or sanctuary was a moveable "tent of meeting" used as a place of sacrifice and worship by the Israelites. At Mount Sinai, God gave His people the law they should follow as well as very specific instructions for the building of the tabernacle. The specifications are recorded in the book of Exodus 25-28, and the requirements of the Levitical priests in their sacrifice within the tabernacle is described in Exodus 35-40. The children of Israel were arranged outside the tabernacle courtyard in specific order, with the Levites situated around the entire structure (Num. 1:53; Num. 2:3-33). The tabernacle symbolized God's dwelling place among His people and served as the center of worship. Technically, the tabernacle was not the entire structure of the courtyard and its contents, but was God's dwelling place in the Holy of Holies. The Hebrew writer speaks of the "first" and the "second" tabernacle, referring to the courtyard structure as the "first" and the Holy Place and Holy of Holies as the "second" (Heb. 9:6-8). Levitical priests would render service in the "first" tabernacle, while the "second" tabernacle was entered only by the High Priest who would offer animal sacrifice for the sins of himself and the people once per year.

THE SPIES AND 40 YEAR WANDERING

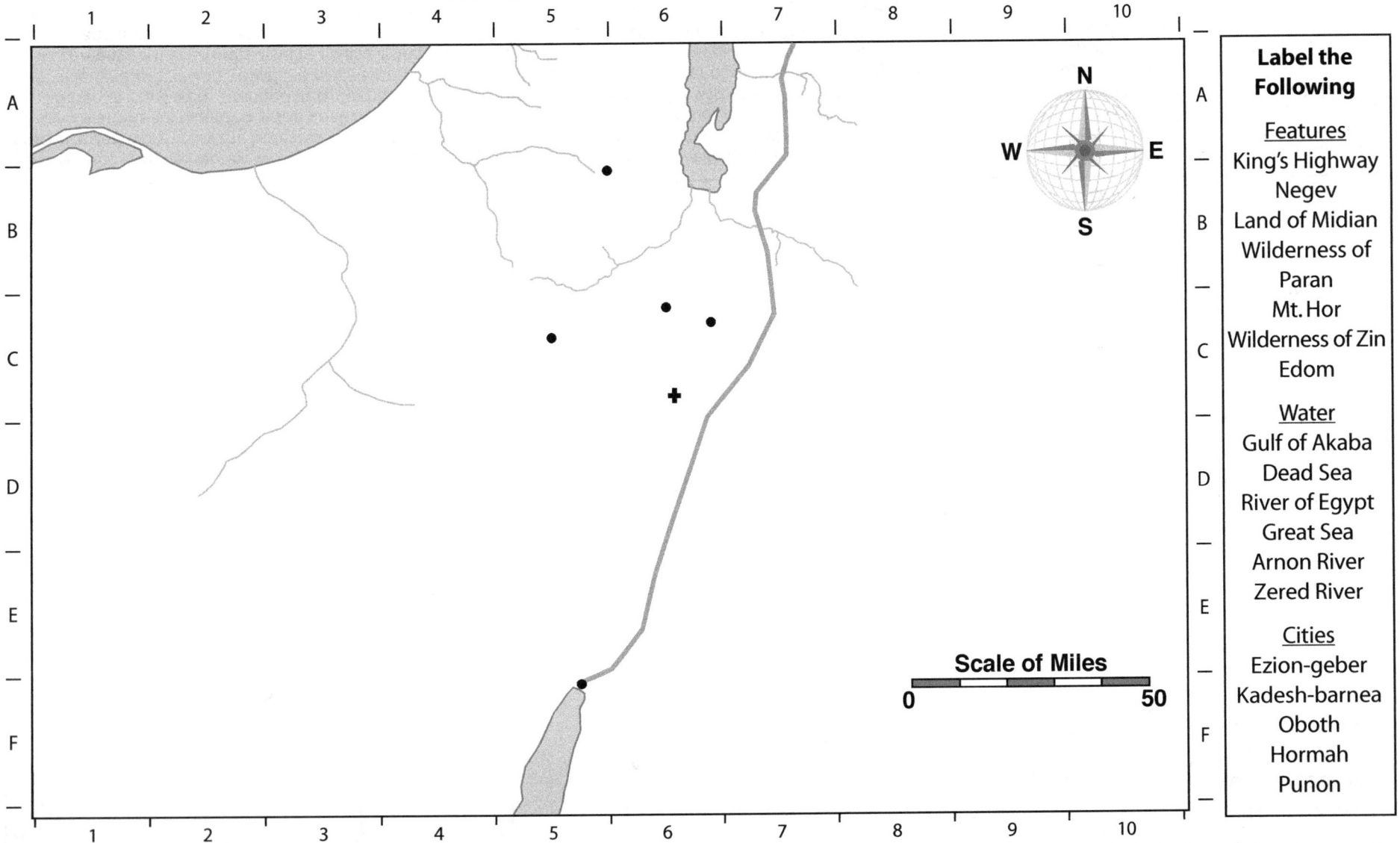

Label the Following

Features
King's Highway
Negev
Land of Midian
Wilderness of Paran
Mt. Hor
Wilderness of Zin
Edom

Water
Gulf of Akaba
Dead Sea
River of Egypt
Great Sea
Arnon River
Zered River

Cities
Ezion-geber
Kadesh-barnea
Oboth
Hormah
Punon

Scale of Miles
0   50

READ THE FOLLOWING: Indicate locations by putting the appropriate letter/number intersection. (Example: A2 is the location of the Great Sea.)

√ **Spies Sent into Canaan** – Numbers 12:16; 13:1-3, 17-33 • Where is the Wilderness of Paran? ___   Where is the Wilderness of Zin? ___

√ **The People Rebel** – Numbers 14:1-4, 26-35, 39-45; Deut. 9:23 • Where is Hormah? ___   Where is Kadesh-barnea? ___

√ **Aaron Dies and More Rebellion** – Numbers 20:22-29; 21:1-10 • Where did Aaron die? ___   Where did God's people confront fiery serpents? ___

4 OLD TESTAMENT GEOGRAPHY
Conquest of Canaan

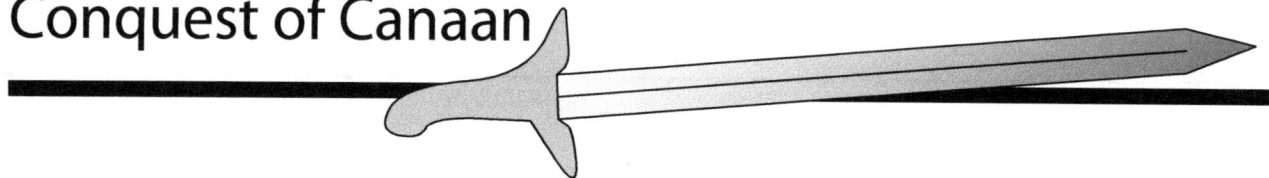

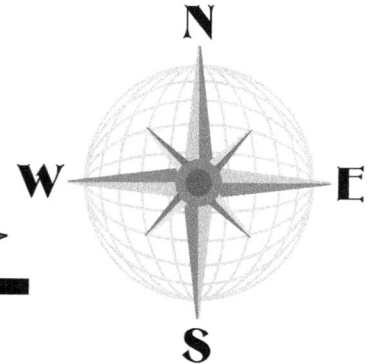

1. Which of the following nations did God say He would destroy so His people could take the promised land (Deut. 7:1-2)?

   A. Amorites   B. Hittites   C. Perizzites   D. Canaanites*

   E. Hivites   F. Jebusites   G. Girgashites

2. List all the reasons why God did not want His people to spare any of the people of the foreign nations. (See Deut 7:3-6.)

   _____

   _____

3. The countries of what two kings did Moses help destroy (Num. 32:33)?

   A. Hazor   B. Og   C. Obed   D. Sihon   E. Dagon

4. From what mount did Moses look into the Promised Land (Deut. 34:1-4)?

   A. Nebo   B. Pisgah   C. Abarim   D. Ebal   E. Gerizim

5. Why was Moses not allowed to enter the Promised Land? (See Num. 20:6-12.)

   _____

6. Circle all the cities burned during the conquest (Josh. 6:24; 8:19; 11:11).

   A. Jericho   B. Ai   C. Hebron   D. Ashdod   E. Hazor

7. According to Deuteronomy 11:26-29 from which mount were curses read and from which were blessings read?
   Mt. Ebal _____   Mt. Gerizim_____

8. What do you think the blessing and cursing represented?

   _____

   _____

9. By what name is the Sea of Galilee called in the Old Testament and in the dividing of Canaan among the tribes (Num. 34:11)?

   A. Sea of Springs   B. Sea of Tiberias   C. Sea of Chinnereth

   D. Tiberian Sea   E. Sea of Gennesaret

10. About how tall do you think Mount Nebo is?
    A. 600 feet   B. 1,600 feet   C. 2,200 feet   D. 2,600 feet

11. Joseph's bones were carried from Egypt and during the 40 year wandering. Where were his bones finally buried? (See Josh 24:32.)

   _____

* It has been suggested that "Canaanites" may have been a general term describing all the nations of the region.

HOSTILE NATIONS IN AND AROUND THE PROMISED LAND

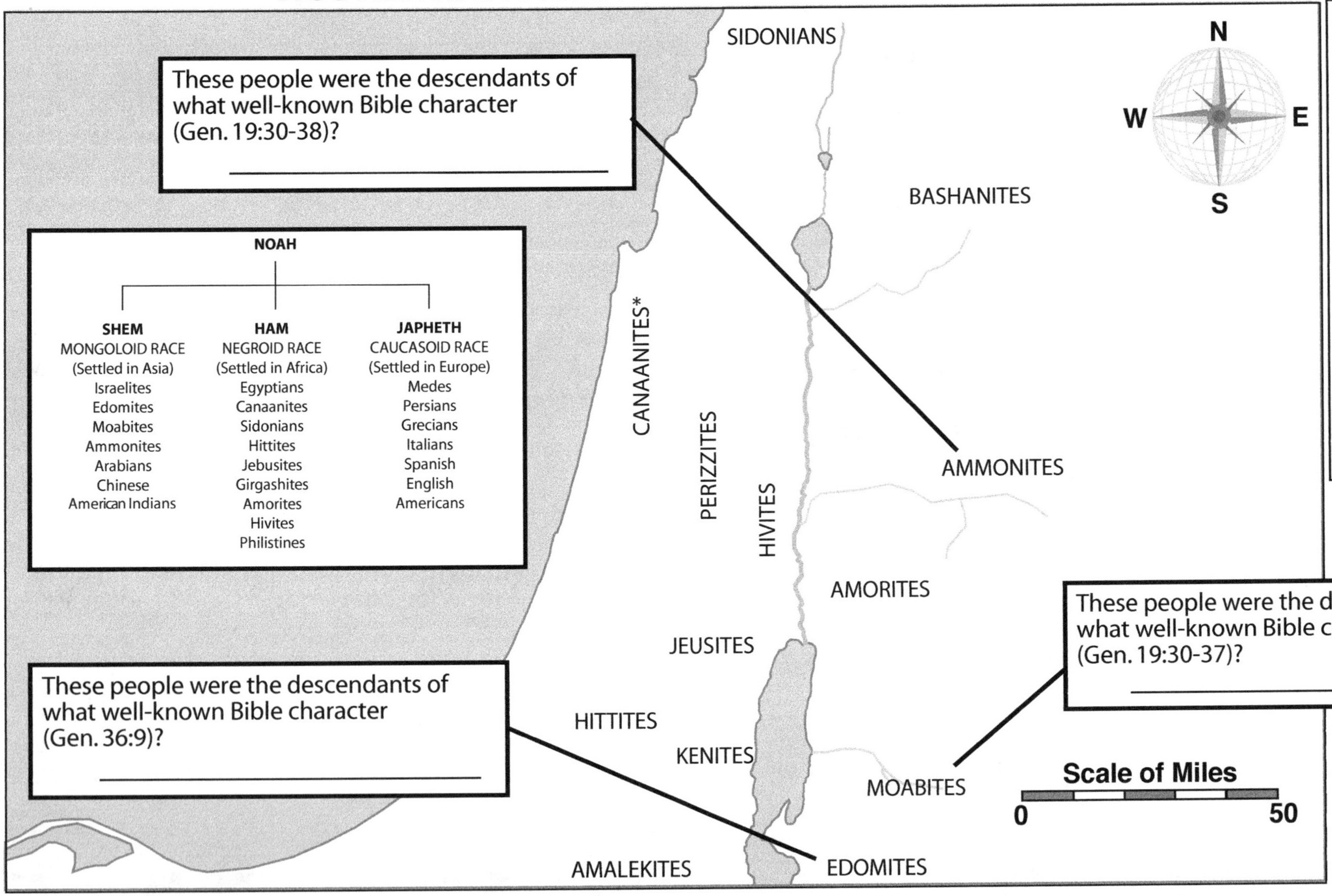

SIDONIANS

These people were the descendants of what well-known Bible character (Gen. 19:30-38)?

_____

BASHANITES

NOAH

SHEM	HAM	JAPHETH
MONGOLOID RACE	NEGROID RACE	CAUCASOID RACE
(Settled in Asia)	(Settled in Africa)	(Settled in Europe)
Israelites	Egyptians	Medes
Edomites	Canaanites	Persians
Moabites	Sidonians	Grecians
Ammonites	Hittites	Italians
Arabians	Jebusites	Spanish
Chinese	Girgashites	English
American Indians	Amorites	Americans
	Hivites	
	Philistines	

CANAANITES*

PERIZZITES

HIVITES

AMMONITES

AMORITES

JEUSITES

These people were the descendants of what well-known Bible character (Gen. 36:9)?

_____

HITTITES

KENITES

These people were the descendants of what well-known Bible character (Gen. 19:30-37)?

_____

MOABITES

Scale of Miles

0   50

AMALEKITES   EDOMITES

Label the Following

<u>Water</u>
Dead Sea
Sea of Galilee
Hula Lake
Great Sea
Jordan River
Yarmuk River
Jabbok River
Arnon River

<u>Feature</u>
Transjordan

READ THE FOLLOWING:

√ **Hostile Nations in Canaan** – Exodus 23:20-33; 34:10-17; Deut. 7:1-6 • What nations did God promise to destroy? List them below:

_____   _____   _____   _____   _____

* It has been suggested that "Canaanites" was a general term used to describe all the nations and people of the region.

THE CONQUEST OF CANAAN

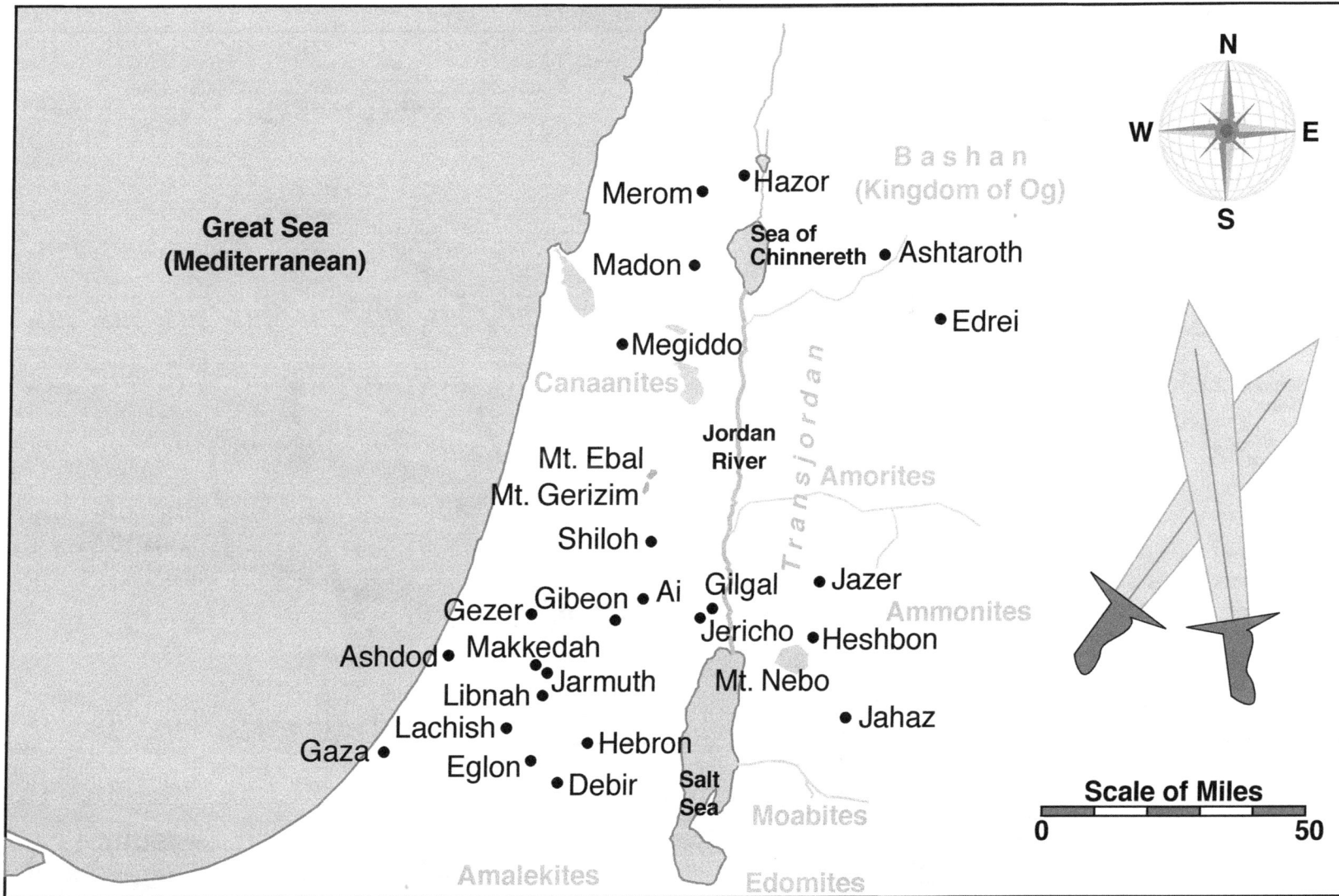

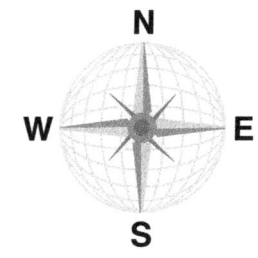

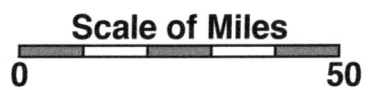

Great Sea
(Mediterranean)

N
W · E
S

Merom ● ●Hazor

Madon ●

Sea of
Chinnereth ●Ashtaroth

B a s h a n
(Kingdom of Og)

●Edrei

●Megiddo

Canaanites

Mt. Ebal

Jordan
River

T r a n s j o r d a n

Amorites

Mt. Gerizim

Shiloh ●

Gezer ● Gibeon ● Ai ● Gilgal ●Jazer

Ammonites

Jericho ●Heshbon

Ashdod ● Makkedah

Jarmuth

Mt. Nebo

Libnah ●

Lachish ● ●Jahaz

Gaza ● Eglon ● ●Hebron

●Debir

Salt
Sea

Moabites

Amalekites

Edomites

Scale of Miles
0 ——————— 50

Do the Following

After reading the passages below, trace Moses's conquest of the Transjordan using a colored pen or pencil.

Next, trace Joshua's conquest of Canaan with a different color.

Circle the three cities that Joshua burned.

Put a box around the location where the five hostile kings hid themselves in a cave.

READ THE FOLLOWING:

√ **Moses' Transjordan Conquest** – Numbers 21:21-35; 27:12-20; Deuteronomy 34:1-8

√ **Joshua's Conquest of Canaan** – Deuteronomy 34:9; Joshua 1:6-7; 6:1-5; 8:24-25, 30-33; 9:3-6; 10:1-11, 16-43; 11:1-23

THE CITY OF JERICHO

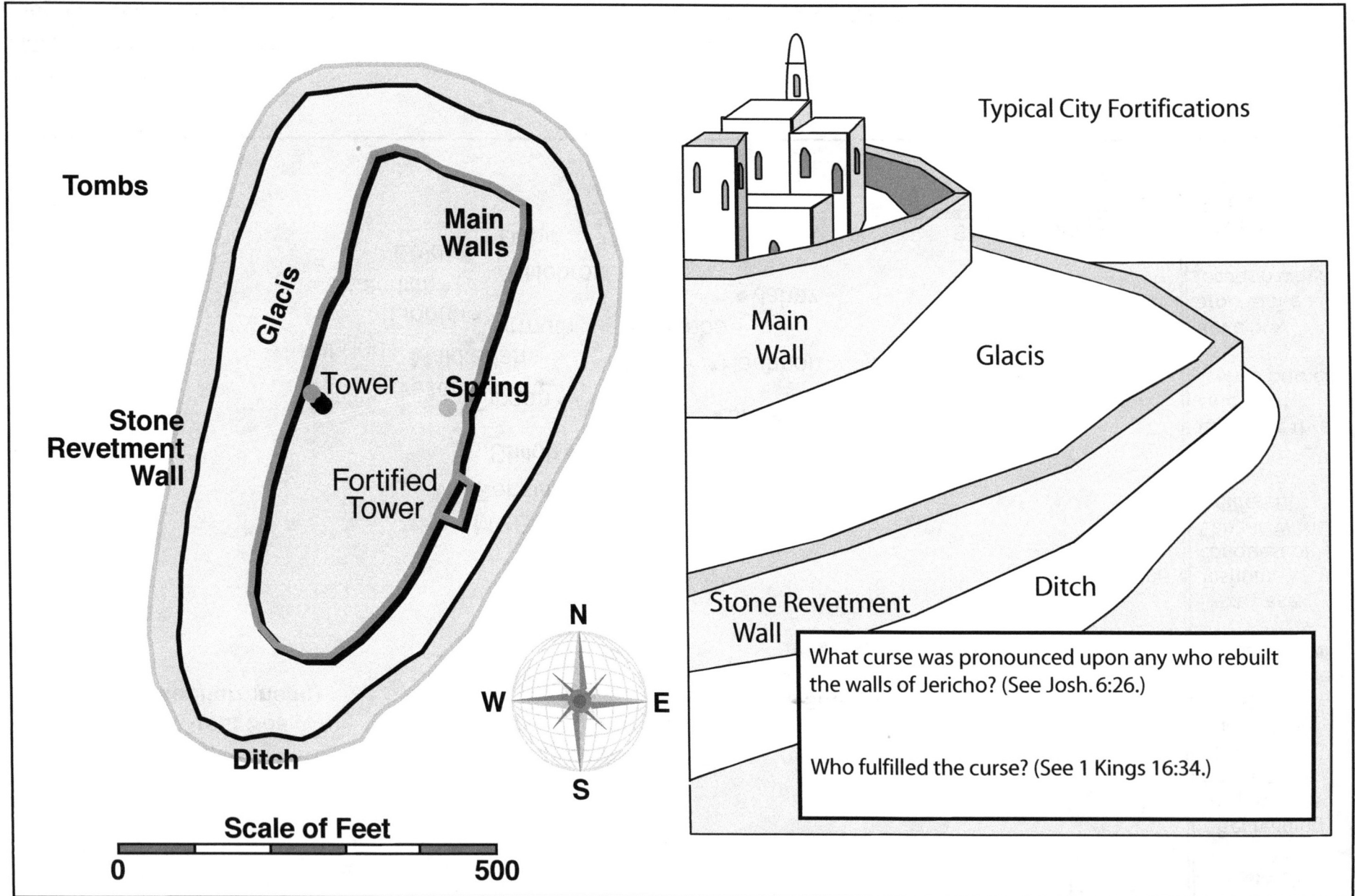

Tombs

Main Walls

Glacis

Tower

Spring

Stone Revetment Wall

Fortified Tower

Ditch

N
W   E
S

Typical City Fortifications

Main Wall

Glacis

Stone Revetment Wall

Ditch

What curse was pronounced upon any who rebuilt the walls of Jericho? (See Josh. 6:26.)

Who fulfilled the curse? (See 1 Kings 16:34.)

Scale of Feet

0   500

5 OLD TESTAMENT GEOGRAPHY
Dividing the Land amongst the Tribes

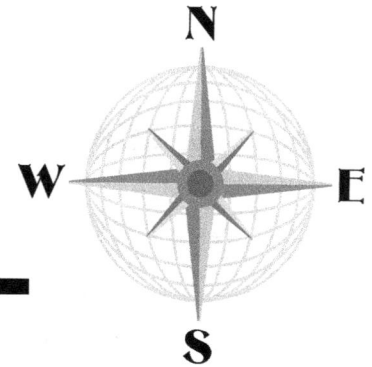

1. What three tribes of Israel ended up with land east of the Jordan River? (See Num. 32:33.)

   _____ _____ _____

2. Which tribes eventually had two land locations? (See the map on page 27.)
   A. Gad   B. Dan   C. Manasseh   D. Asher   E. Zebulun

3. Which tribe eventually was absorbed by the tribe of Judah? (Hint: It lay to the south of Judah.)
   A. Simeon   B. Reuben   C. Benjamin   D. Ephraim   E. Gad

4. Which of Jacob's sons did **not** receive a tribal allocation named after himself?
   A. Asher   B. Joseph   C. Gad   E. Issachar   F. Dan

5. The city of Jerusalem was located on the border of what two tribes? (See Chron. 11:1.)
   A. Judah   B. Simeon   C. Dan   D. Reuben   E. Benjamin

6. Through which of Jacob's sons did the lineage of Christ pass (Matt. 1:2-3)?
   A. Benjamin   B. Asher   C. Judah   D. Joseph   E. Levi

7. Which of Jacob's sons listed below did **not** receive a tribal allocation of land like that of his brothers? (See Josh. 13:14.)
   A. Simeon   B. Levi   C. Dan   D. Asher   E. Zebulun

8. What inheritance did the tribe of Levi receive? (See Josh. 13:33.)

   _____

9. Which of the tribes received the largest single land allocation? (See the map on page 23.)
   A. Issachar   B. Reuben   C. Naphtali   D. Manasseh   E. Judah

10. During the time of the conquest, what predominated the area of Canaan? (See 1 Sam. 22:5 for a hint.)
    A. Desert   B. Grasslands   C. Forests   D. Sand dunes

11. Which tribe extended the furthest southward?
    A. Simeon   B. Judah   C. Gad   D. Reuben   E. Benjamin

12. Which tribe extended the furthest eastward?
    A. Reuben   B. Gad   C. Manasseh   D. Dan   E. Judah

13. Which tribe's land area is illustrated below?

    _____

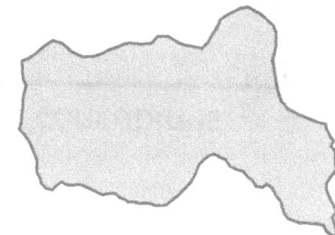

THE DESCENDANTS OF JACOB

INSTRUCTIONS: Read the passages below, and then complete the chart by putting names under each of the figures.

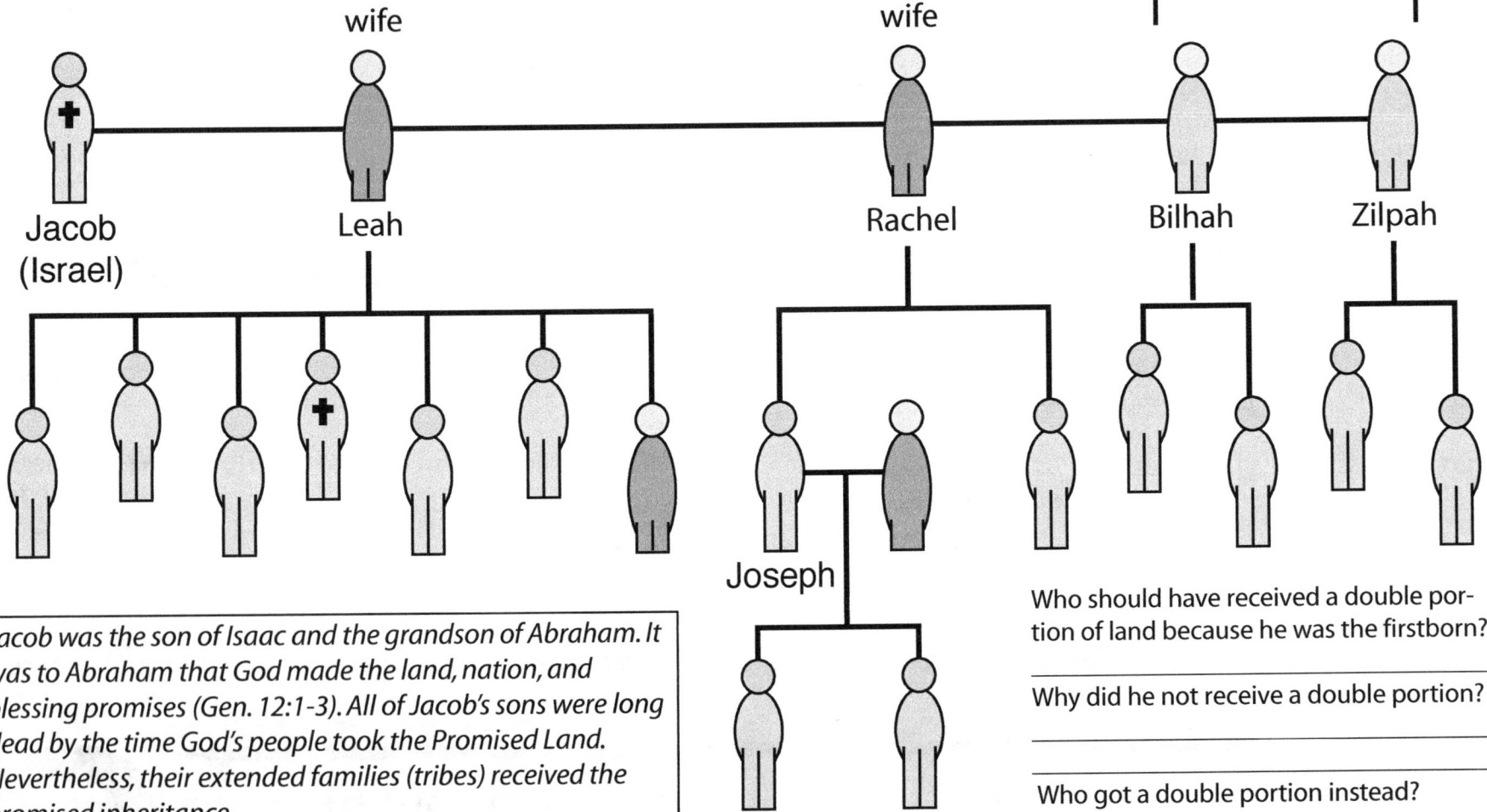

concubines

wife

wife

Jacob
(Israel)

Leah

Rachel

Bilhah

Zilpah

Joseph

Jacob was the son of Isaac and the grandson of Abraham. It was to Abraham that God made the land, nation, and blessing promises (Gen. 12:1-3). All of Jacob's sons were long dead by the time God's people took the Promised Land. Nevertheless, their extended families (tribes) received the promised inheritance.

Who should have received a double portion of land because he was the firstborn?

_____

Why did he not receive a double portion?

_____

_____

Who got a double portion instead?

_____

† indicates lineage of Christ

READ THE FOLLOWING:

√ **Jacob's Wives/Handmaids and Offspring** – Genesis 29:21-35, 30:1-24; 35:17-18; 41:50-52; 49:1-34

THE TWELVE TRIBES OF ISRAEL

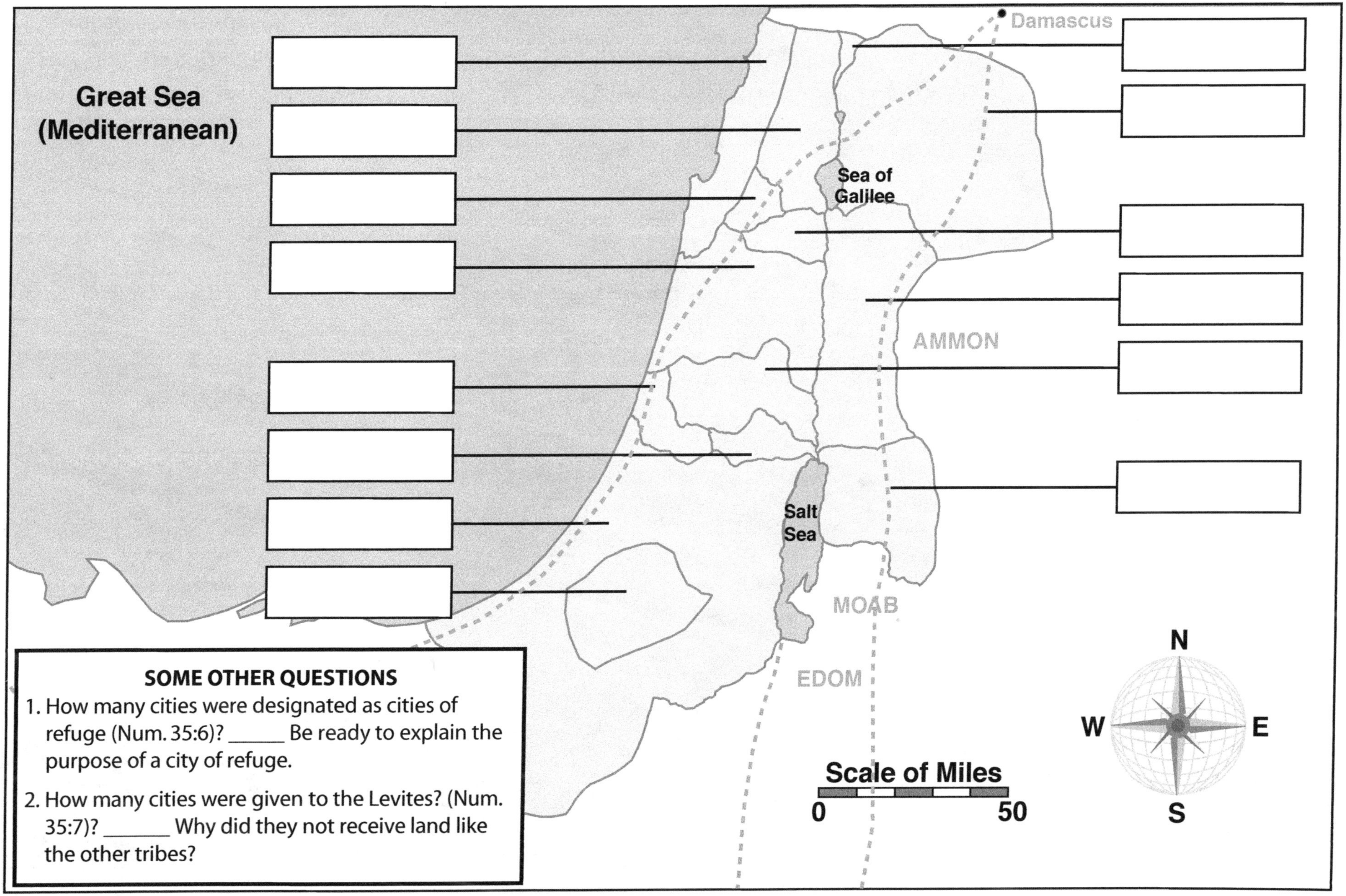

**Great Sea
(Mediterranean)**

Damascus

Sea of
Galilee

AMMON

Salt
Sea

MOAB

EDOM

N

W   E

S

Scale of Miles

0   50

SOME OTHER QUESTIONS

1. How many cities were designated as cities of
   refuge (Num. 35:6)? _____ Be ready to explain the
   purpose of a city of refuge.

2. How many cities were given to the Levites? (Num.
   35:7)? _____ Why did they not receive land like
   the other tribes?

INSTRUCTIONS: Complete the map above by filling in the boxes with the name of each tribe. Label the three major highways represented by the dashed lines.

© 2020 Truth Publications, Inc.

A LAND FLOWING WITH "MILK AND HONEY"

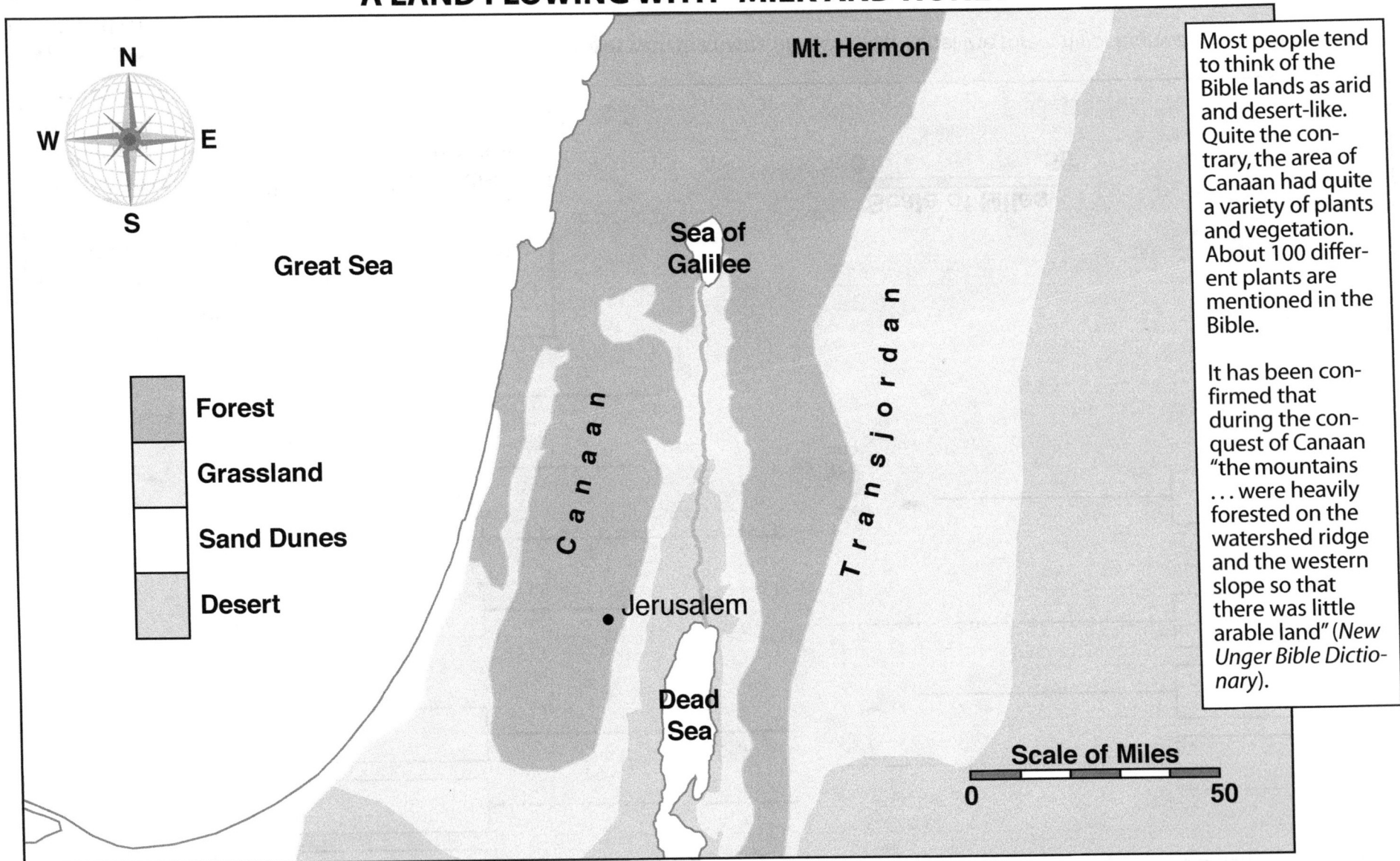

N **W** **E** **S**

Great Sea

Mt. Hermon

Sea of
Galilee

C a n a a n

T r a n s j o r d a n

Forest

Grassland

Sand Dunes

Desert

● Jerusalem

Dead
Sea

Most people tend
to think of the
Bible lands as arid
and desert-like.
Quite the con-
trary, the area of
Canaan had quite
a variety of plants
and vegetation.
About 100 differ-
ent plants are
mentioned in the
Bible.

It has been con-
firmed that
during the con-
quest of Canaan
"the mountains
. . . were heavily
forested on the
watershed ridge
and the western
slope so that
there was little
arable land" (*New
Unger Bible Dictio-
nary*).

Scale of Miles

0   50

READ THE FOLLOWING:

√ **Arid or Forested?** 1 Samuel 22:5; and 2 Chronicles 27:4 • What is mentioned in these verses about vegetation? _____

√ **Some Varieties of Trees** - Exodus 25:10; Ecclesiastes12:5; Song of Solomon 2:3; Judges 3:13; 9:15; Zecheriah 11:2 • What trees are specifically

mentioned? List them here: _____

6 OLD TESTAMENT GEOGRAPHY
The Period of the Judges (about 1370–1030 BC)

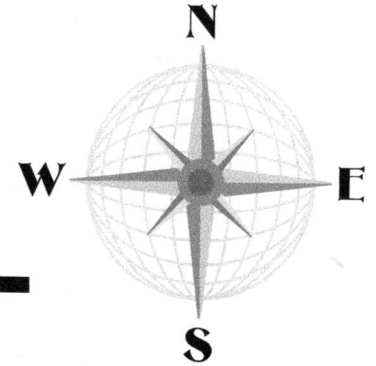

1. Who was the first judge? (See Judg. 3:9.)
   A. Shamgar   B. Othniel   C. Ehud   D. Gideon   E. Eli

2. Who was the only female judge (Judg. 4:4)?

   _____

3. Who was the last judge of Israel (1 Sam. 7:15)?
   A. Abdon   B. Tola   C. Elon   E. Samuel   F. Jair

4. Caleb along with Joshua was one of the two spies who urged God's people to take the promised land. His nephew was a judge. Who was he (Judg. 3:9)?
   A. Shamgar   B. Othniel   C. Ehud   D. Gideon   E. Eli

5. This judge plunged a dagger so deeply into the belly of the fat king of Eglon, that he could not withdraw it (Judg. 3:15-22):
   A. Shamgar   B. Othniel   C. Ehud   D. Ibzan   E. Tola

6. This judge killed 600 Philistines with an ox goad (Judg. 3:31):
   A. Samson   B. Samuel   C. Shamgar   D. Jair   E. Eli

7. Name two judges who were also prophets (Judg. 4:4; 1 Sam. 3:20):

   _____   _____

8. This judge asked for signs from God on three occasions before he and his troops routed the Midianites with trumpets, pitchers and torches (Judg. 7:20):
   A. Gideon   B. Othniel   C. Deborah   D. Ibzan   E. Tola

9. This judge was known for his great physical strength (Judg. 16:6):
   A. Gideon   B. Othniel   C. Samson   D. Ibzan   E. Samuel

10. This judge did not "restrain" his sons who were very wicked (1 Sam. 3:13-14):
    A. Eli   B. Othniel   C. Ehud   D. Ibzan   E. Tola

11. Put the judges in order from first to last:

    Othniel ____
    Samson ____
    Ibzan ____
    Deborah ____
    Eli ____
    Gideon ____
    Samuel ____
    Tola ____
    Ehud ____
    Shamgar ____
    Abdon ____
    Jephthah ____
    Elon ____
    Jair ____

JUDGES TIMELINE

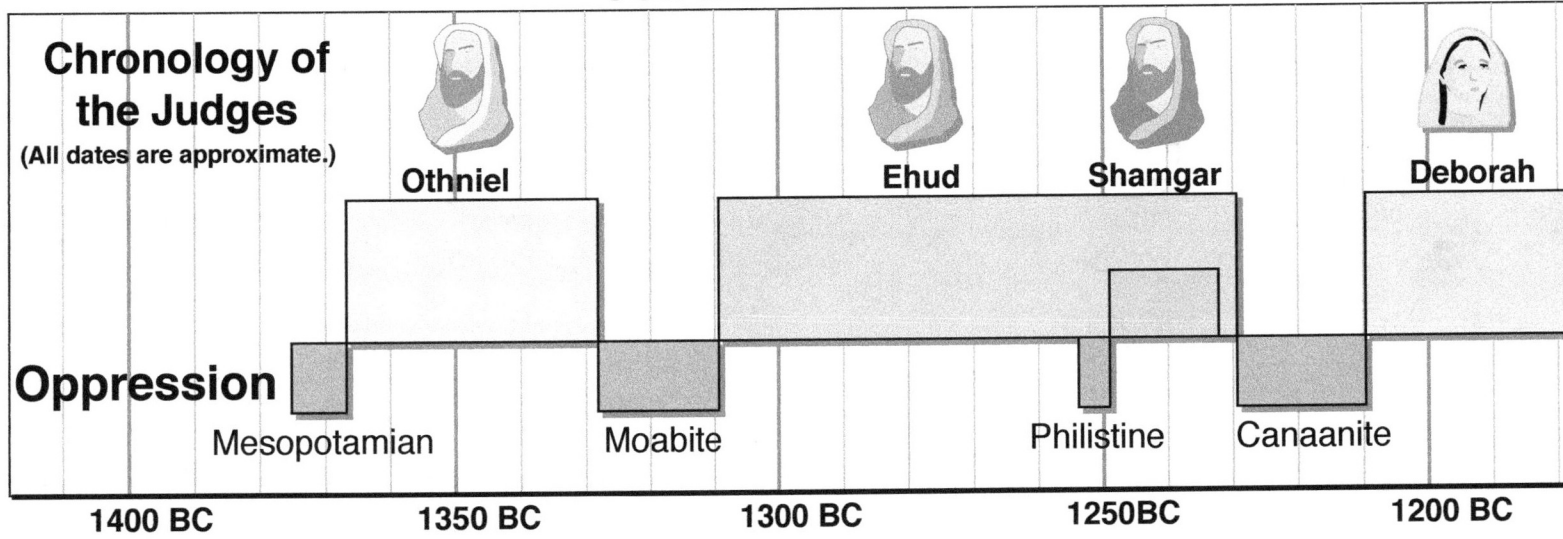

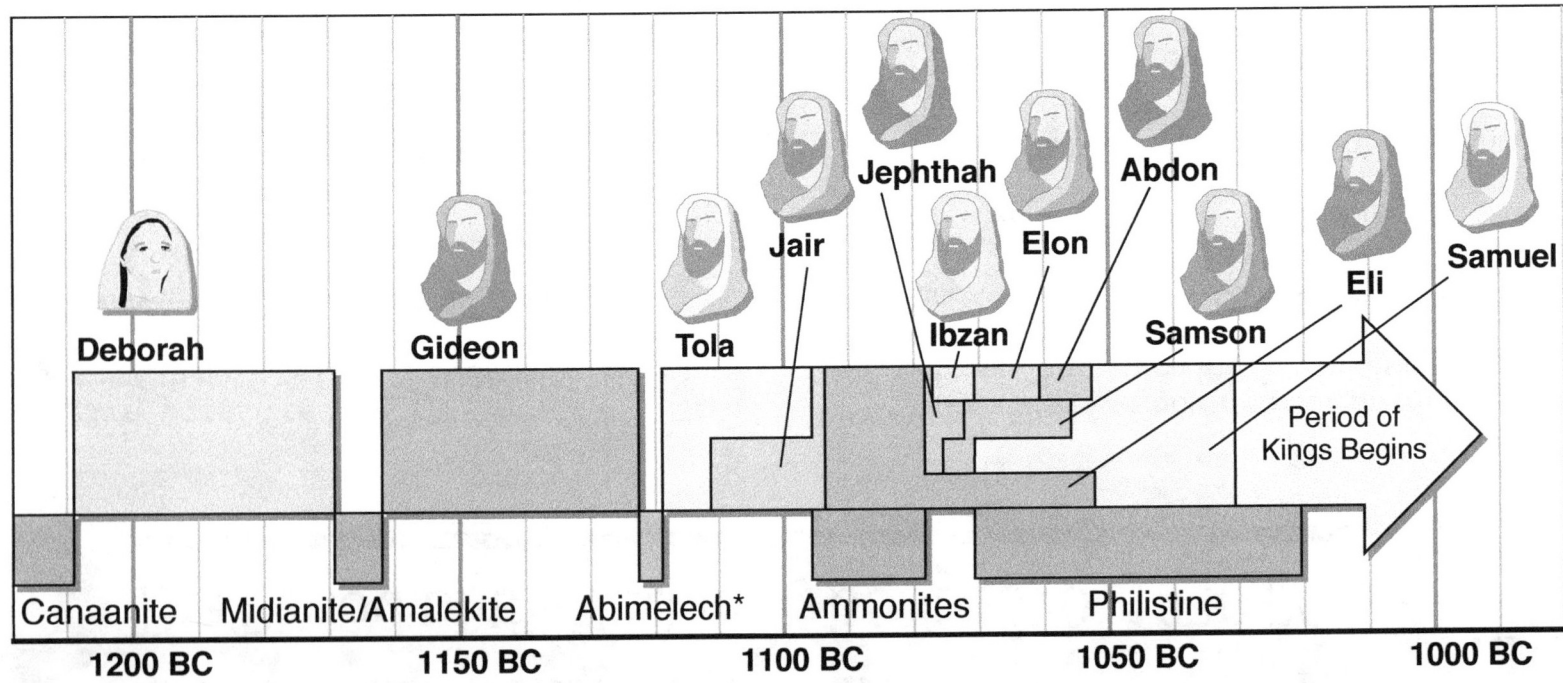

Chronology of the Judges
(All dates are approximate.)

Othniel   Ehud   Shamgar   Deborah

Oppression

Mesopotamian   Moabite   Philistine   Canaanite

1400 BC   1350 BC   1300 BC   1250BC   1200 BC

Deborah   Gideon   Tola   Jair   Jephthah   Ibzan   Elon   Abdon   Samson   Eli   Samuel

Period of Kings Begins

Canaanite   Midianite/Amalekite   Abimelech*   Ammonites   Philistine

1200 BC   1150 BC   1100 BC   1050 BC   1000 BC

READ THE FOLLOWING:

√ **Was Abimelech a Judge? Read Judges 9.**

Some books have Abimelech as a judge, whereas the chart above displays him as an oppressor. Which is it? Be ready to defend your answer.

OPPRESSIONS DURING THE JUDGES

INSTRUCTIONS: On the line provided, write in the name of the judge who arose to deliver Israel from each of the oppressions indicated on this map.

QUESTION: Why did God allow His people to be oppressed by foreign nations? Be ready to provide Scriptures to support your answer.

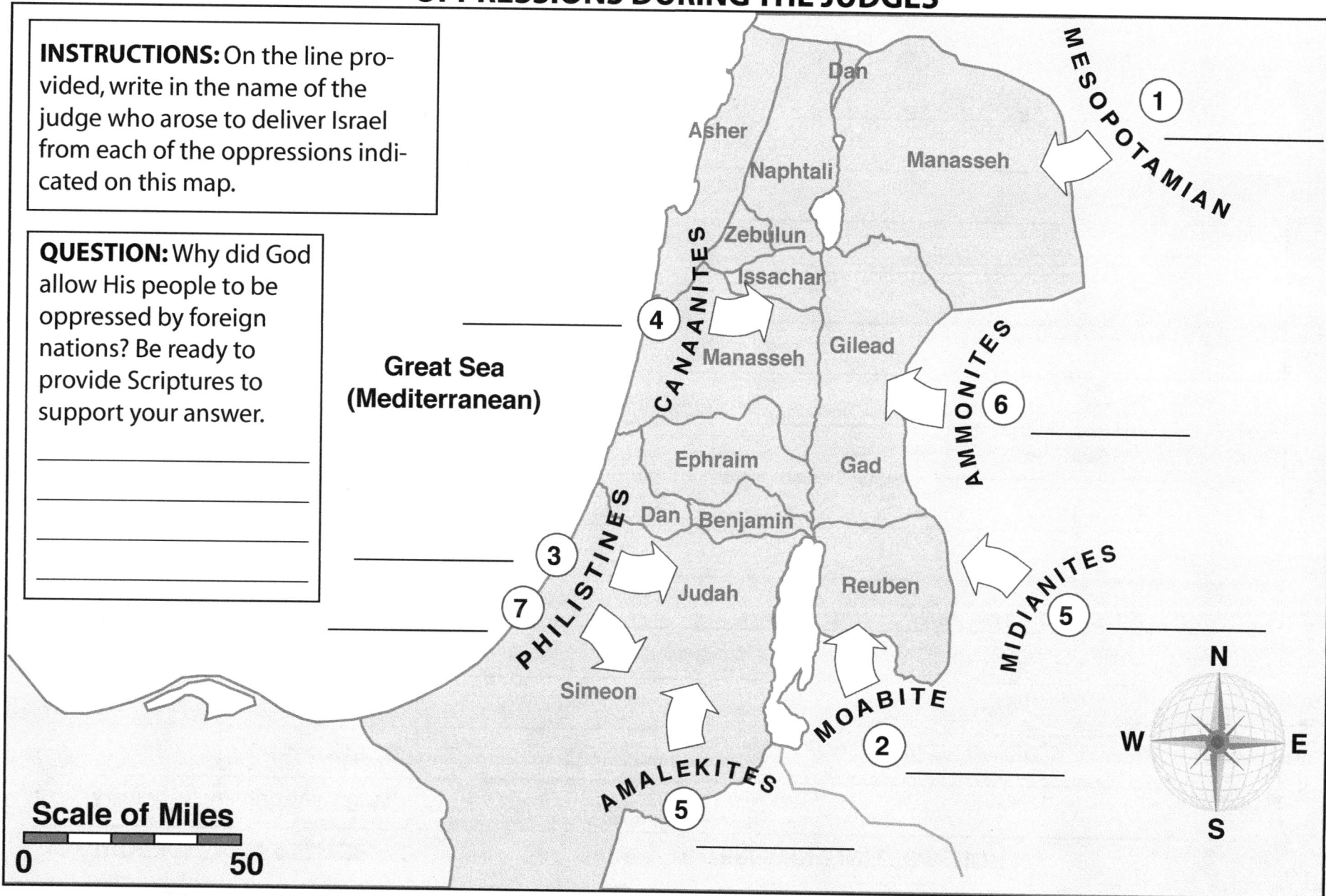

_____

_____

_____

_____

MESOPOTAMIAN

① _____

Dan

Asher

Naphtali

Manasseh

Zebulun

Issachar

④ _____

CANAANITES

Manasseh

Gilead

Great Sea (Mediterranean)

AMMONITES

⑥ _____

Ephraim

Gad

Dan   Benjamin

③ _____

PHILISTINES

Judah

Reuben

MIDIANITES

⑦ _____

⑤ _____

Simeon

MOABITE

② _____

AMALEKITES

⑤ _____

N

W   E

S

Scale of Miles

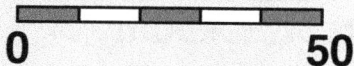

0   50

READ THE FOLLOWING:

√ **Deborah – A Female Judge (Judges 4)**

God typically chose men to be judges. Why do you think God chose Deborah to be a judge in Israel?

MORE ABOUT THE JUDGES

INSTRUCTIONS: Read the passages and provide some tidbit of information about each of the judges.

JUDGE	PASSAGE	INTERESTING INFORMATION
Othniel	Judges 3:8-11	
Ehud	Judges 3:15-22	
Shamgar	Judges 3:31	
Deborah	Judges 4:4-7	
Gideon	Judges 6:17-40	
Tola	Judges 10:1-2	
Jair	Judges 10:3-5	
Jephthah	Judges 11, 12	
Ibzan	Judges 12:8-10	
Elon	Judges 12:11-12	
Abdon	Judges 12:13-15	
Samson	Judges 13-16	
Eli	1 Samuel 4:12-18	
Samuel	1 Samuel 3:1-18	

OLD TESTAMENT GEOGRAPHY
The United Kingdom of Israel – Part 1

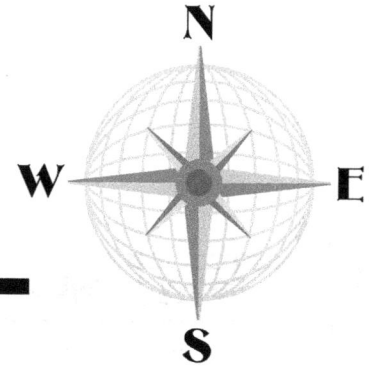

1. Who was the first king to reign over Israel (1 Sam. 8:7; 11:15)?
   A. David   B. Samuel   C. Saul   D. Solomon   E. None of the above

2. Why did God's people want a king (1 Sam. 8:4-5)?

   _____

3. What unique physical feature is mentioned in the Bible about king Saul (1 Sam. 10:23)?

   _____

4. What did king Saul do that caused him to lose the kingdom? (See 1 Sam. 13:8-14; 15:1-26.)

   _____

   _____

   _____

5. Circle the kings who ruled *before* Solomon (2 Sam. 2:8-10).
   A. David   B. Saul   C. Ishbosheth   D. Jeroboam   E. Ahab

6. What city was also known as the "City of David" (2 Sam. 5:7; 20:6; Luke 2:4)?
   A. Hebron   B. Jerusalem   C. Bethlehem   D. Gibeon   E. Gath

7. What spring is situated just outside the walls of Jerusalem? (See page 32.)
   A. Spring of Harod   B. Gihon   C. Gibeah   D. Gushing

8. Who occupied the city of Jerusalem before David defeated it? (See 1 Chron. 11:4.)
   A. Hivites   B. Hittites   C. Kenites   D. Girgashites   E. Jebusites

9. Who became commander and chief of David's armies for his act of heroism in taking the city of Jebus (1 Chron. 11:5-6)?
   A. Joab   B. Rechab   C. Baanah   D. Jereb   E. Hiram

10. About when do you think David ruled as king of Israel?
    A. 1500 BC   B. 1000 BC   C. 500 BC   D. 100 BC

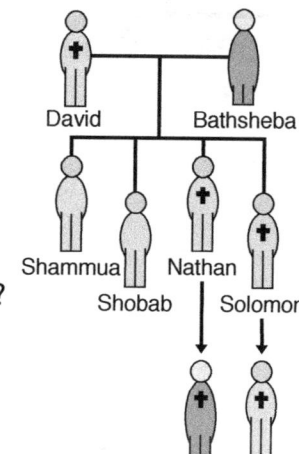

What woman could trace her lineage through Nathan to David (Luke 3:23-31)?

_____

What man could trace his lineage through Solomon to David (Matt. 1:2-16)?

_____

David — Bathsheba
Shammua   Shobab   Nathan   Solomon

✝ indicates lineage of Christ

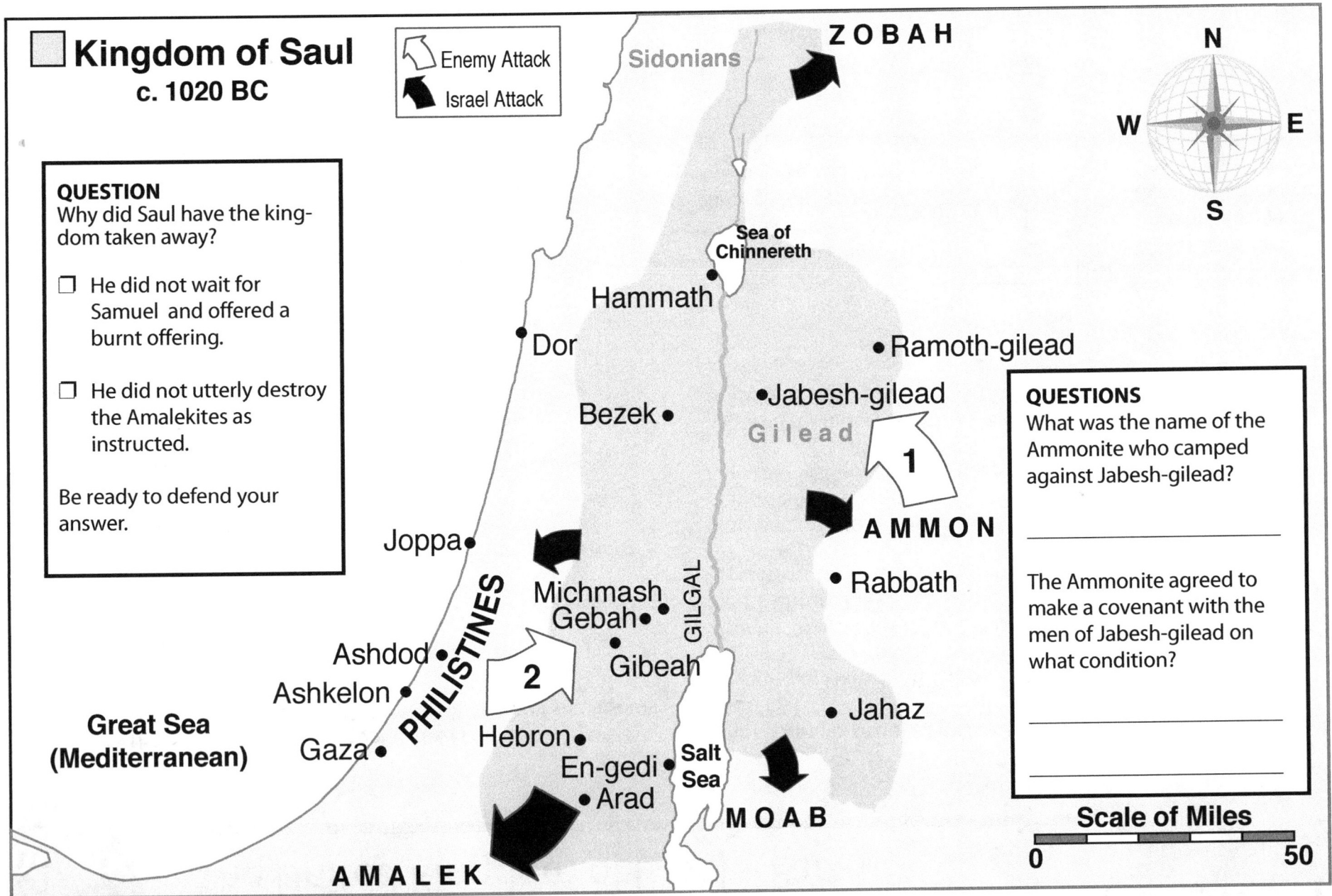

Kingdom of Saul
c. 1020 BC

Enemy Attack
Israel Attack

ZOBAH

Sidonians

QUESTION
Why did Saul have the king-dom taken away?

☐ He did not wait for Samuel and offered a burnt offering.

☐ He did not utterly destroy the Amalekites as instructed.

Be ready to defend your answer.

Sea of Chinnereth

Hammath

Dor

• Ramoth-gilead

• Jabesh-gilead

Bezek •

Gilead

1

QUESTIONS
What was the name of the Ammonite who camped against Jabesh-gilead?

_____

The Ammonite agreed to make a covenant with the men of Jabesh-gilead on what condition?

_____

_____

Joppa •

AMMON

Michmash

Gebah •

GILGAL

• Rabbath

PHILISTINES

Gibeah

Ashdod •

2

Ashkelon •

Great Sea (Mediterranean)

Hebron •

• Jahaz

Gaza •

En-gedi •

Salt Sea

• Arad

MOAB

Scale of Miles

0   50

AMALEK

READ THE FOLLOWING TO HELP YOU WITH THE ANSWERS ABOVE.
√ 1 Samuel 8:4-22; 11:1-15; 13:1-14; 14:47; 15:1-35

CITY OF DAVID
circa 1000 BC

North Gate
Valley Gate
Millo?
Citadel
Mt. Zion
Tsinnor?
Water Gate
Pool Tower
Spring Tower
Gihon Spring
Pool
Tyropoeon Valley
Kidron Valley
Tomb of David
Fountain Gate

Scale of Feet
0   500

Kingdom of David
c. 1000 BC

N
W   E
S

Tyre
Sidonians

Sea of Chinnereth
Aphek
Hammath
Megiddo
Jabesh-gilead
Jordan River
GILEAD
☆ Mahanaim
AMMON
Rabbath

David drove the Philistines into a relatively small area.

Gibeon
☆ Jebus
Ashdod
Gath
Bethlehem
Ashkelon
Hebron ☆
Jahaz
Gaza
PHILISTINES

Great Sea (Mediterranean)

Salt Sea

MOAB

© 1999 MANNA

AMALEK
Aroer

Scale of Miles
0   50

QUESTIONS
Was Israel a divided kingdom during David's reign?
__ Yes __ No
Who ruled from Mahanaim?

_____

Who ruled from Hebron?

_____

Who moved the center of power to Jerusalem?

_____

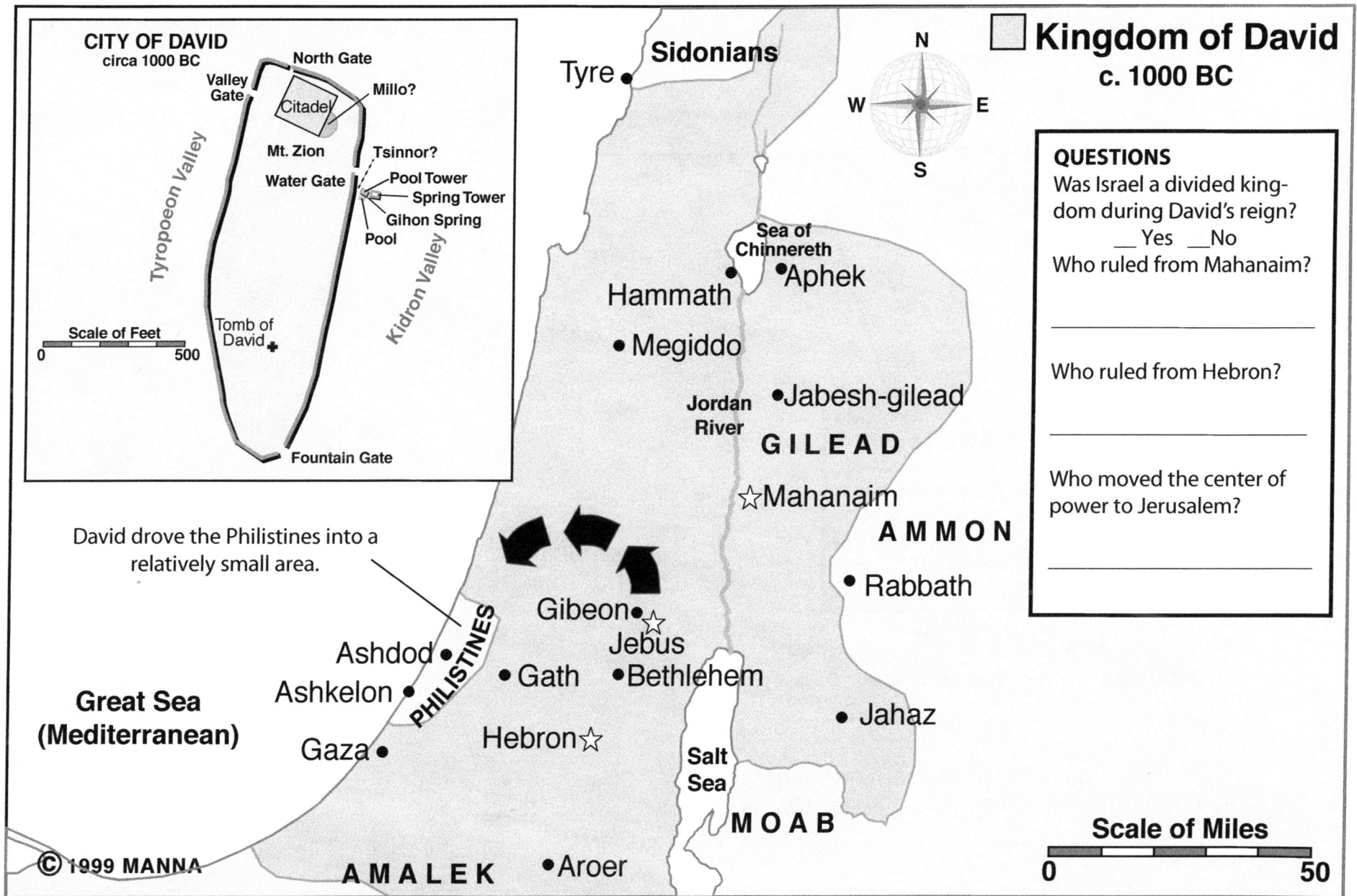

READ THE FOLLOWING TO HELP YOU WITH THE ANSWERS ABOVE.
√ 2 Samuel 2:1-11; 3:1; 5:1-10

Jebus Water System

The "gutter" or "water tunnel" (Hebrew *tsinnor*) mentioned as the means whereby David's forces entered the city has been the subject of much archaeological investigation.

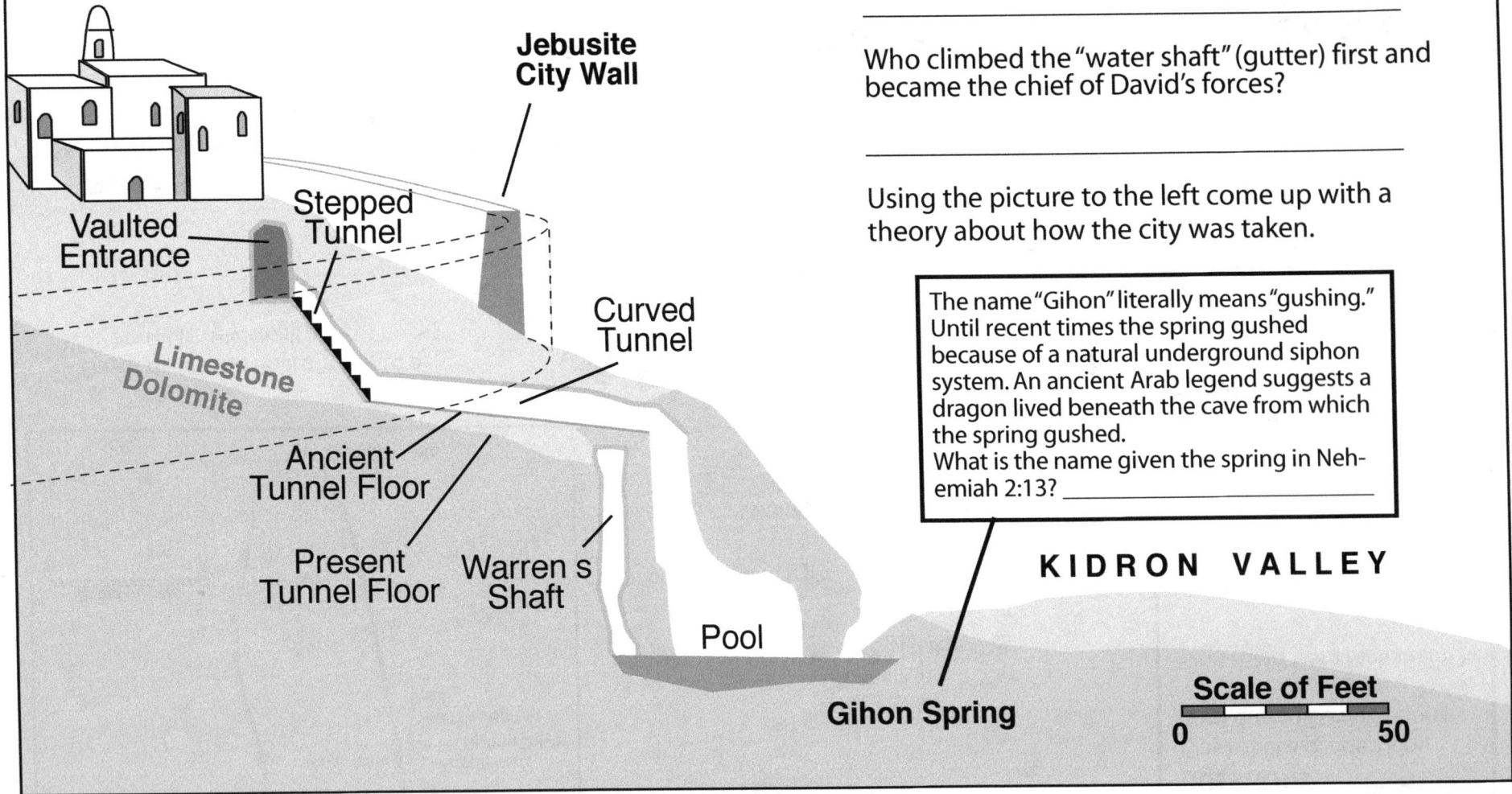

Vaulted Entrance

Stepped Tunnel

Jebusite City Wall

Curved Tunnel

Limestone Dolomite

Ancient Tunnel Floor

Present Tunnel Floor

Warren's Shaft

Pool

Gihon Spring

KIDRON VALLEY

QUESTIONS

What did the inhabitants of Jebus say to taunt David and his forces?

_____

_____

Who climbed the "water shaft" (gutter) first and became the chief of David's forces?

_____

Using the picture to the left come up with a theory about how the city was taken.

The name "Gihon" literally means "gushing." Until recent times the spring gushed because of a natural underground siphon system. An ancient Arab legend suggests a dragon lived beneath the cave from which the spring gushed.

What is the name given the spring in Nehemiah 2:13? _____

Scale of Feet

0   50

READ THE FOLLOWING TO HELP YOU WITH THE ANSWER ABOVE

√ 2 Samuel 5:6-8; 1 Chronicles 11:4-7

LESSON 8

OLD TESTAMENT GEOGRAPHY
The United Kingdom of Israel – Part 2

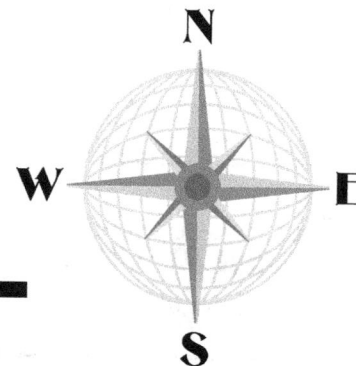

1. Which of David's sons became king when David died (1 Kings 2:10-12)?
   A. Amnon   B. Absalom   C. Adonijah   D. Solomon

2. Who was the mother of the king that replaced David (1 Kings 1:11)?
   A. Michal   B. Bathsheba   C. Abigail   D. Haggith

3. Where was Solomon when the Lord appeared to him and told him to ask for whatever he wished (1 Kings 3:4-14)?
   A. Gibeon   B. Ekron   C. Jerusalem   D. Shechem   E. Gaza

4. For what did Solomon ask? _____
   _____
   _____

5. What did the Lord give Solomon? _____
   _____
   _____

6. What condition did the Lord place upon Solomon in return for prolonging his days (1 Kings 3:14)?
   _____
   _____

7. Where was Solomon when two woman came to him claiming the be the mother of the same child (1 Kings 3:15-28)?
   A. Gibeon   B. Ekron   C. Jerusalem   D. Shechem   E. Gaza

8. What was the extent of Solomon's kingdom (1 Kings 4:21-28)?
   _____

9. Solomon formed a trade agreement with the king of what area (1 Kings 3:1-2; 5:1-12)?
   A. Tyre   B. Egypt   C. Arabia   D. Cyprus   E. Ammon

10. Where did Solomon send 10,000 forced laborers every month to cut cedar and cypress trees (1 Kings 5:8-14)?
    A. Egypt   B. Babylon   C. Crete   D. Lebanon   E. Arabia

11. Besides many building projects, where did Solomon build fortress (walled) cities (1 Kings 9:15)?
    A. Jerusalem   B. Hazor   C. Megiddo   D. Gezer   E. Rabbah

12. The Queen of Sheba came to visit Solomon to test his knowledge and see his wealth (1 Kings 10:1-10). Where is Sheba?
    A. Ethiopia   B. Arabia   C. India   D. Location not known

13. Where did Solomon get some of his wives (1 Kings 11:1-13)?
    A. Egypt   B. Moab   C. Ammon   D. Edom   E. Sidon   F. Hittite

14. Was Solomon a "good" or "evil" king? Be ready to defend your answer.

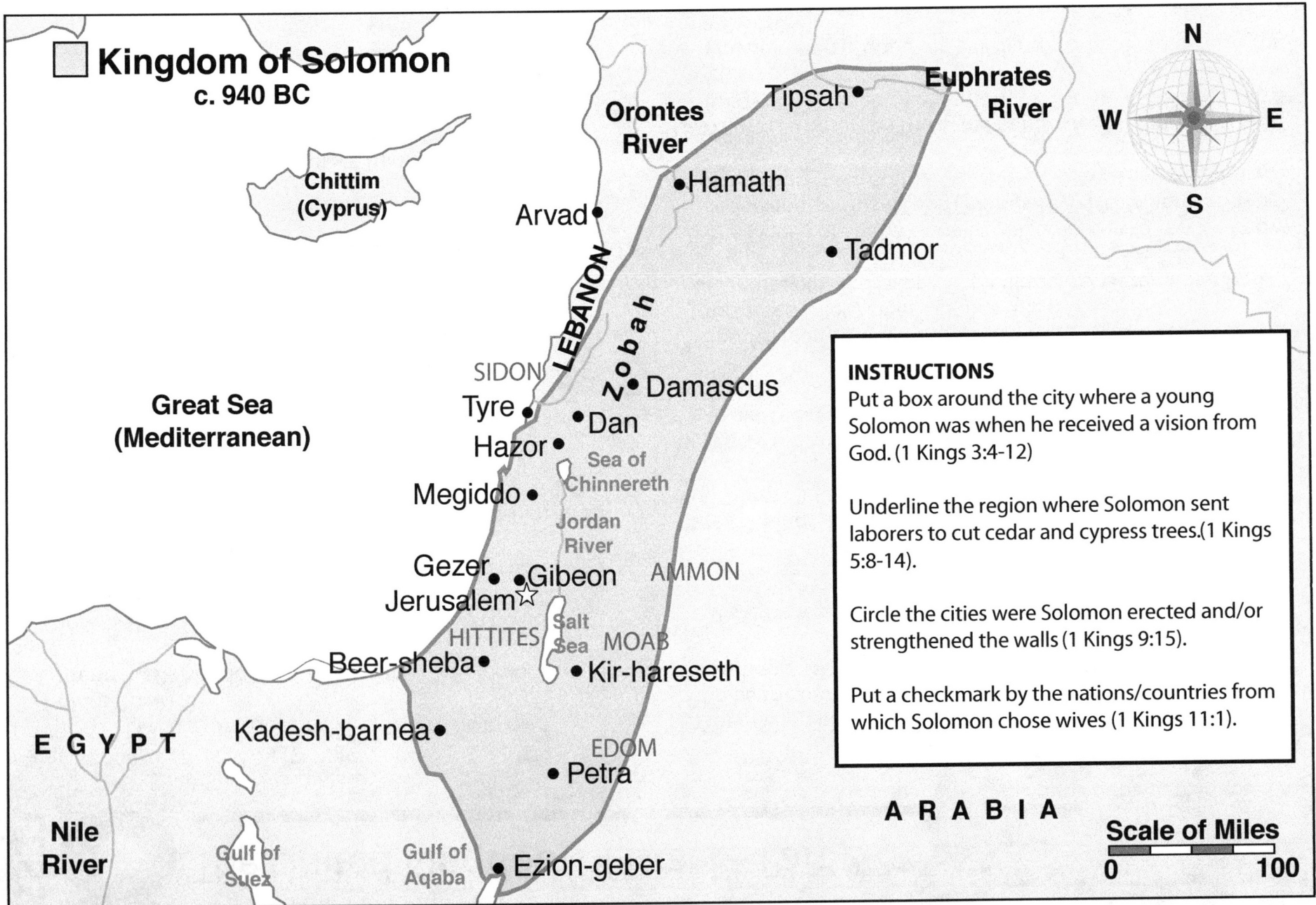

Kingdom of Solomon
c. 940 BC

Chittim (Cyprus)

Great Sea (Mediterranean)

Orontes River

Tipsah •

Euphrates River

• Hamath

Arvad •

• Tadmor

LEBANON

Zobah

SIDON

Damascus •

Tyre •

• Dan

Hazor •

Sea of Chinnereth

Megiddo •

Jordan River

AMMON

Gezer •

• Gibeon

Jerusalem ☆

Salt Sea

HITTITES

MOAB

Beer-sheba •

• Kir-hareseth

Kadesh-barnea •

EDOM

EGYPT

• Petra

ARABIA

Nile River

Gulf of Suez

Gulf of Aqaba

• Ezion-geber

INSTRUCTIONS
Put a box around the city where a young Solomon was when he received a vision from God. (1 Kings 3:4-12)

Underline the region where Solomon sent laborers to cut cedar and cypress trees.(1 Kings 5:8-14).

Circle the cities were Solomon erected and/or strengthened the walls (1 Kings 9:15).

Put a checkmark by the nations/countries from which Solomon chose wives (1 Kings 11:1).

Scale of Miles

0   100

Jerusalem
Expanded by Solomon
circa 950 BC

Keeping in mind that a *royal* cubit was about 20.5 inches in length, what was the square footage of the temple? (See 1 Kings 6:2.)

_____ Square feet

What was the square footage of Solomon's palace? (See 1 Kings 7:2.)

_____ Square feet

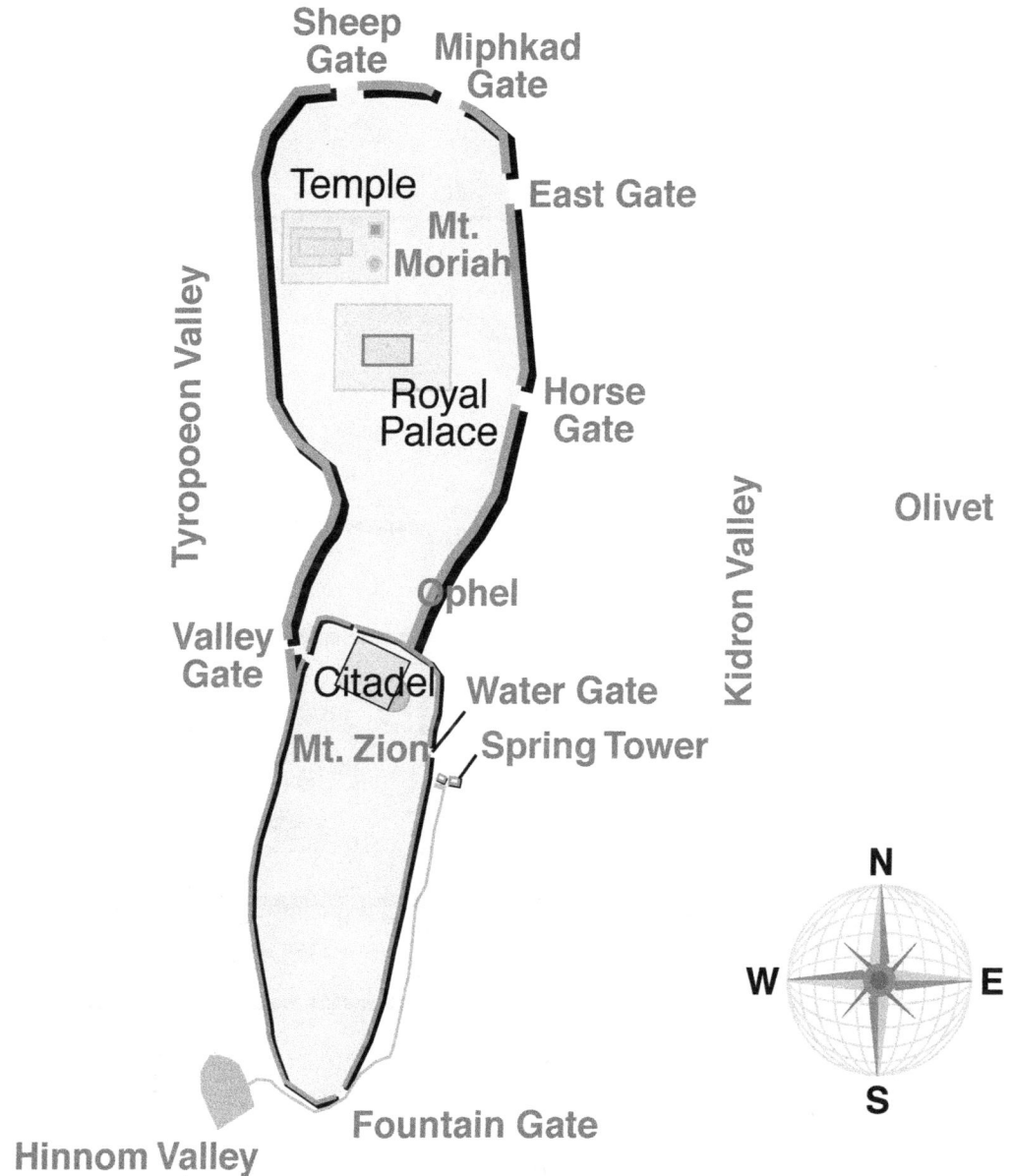

Sheep Gate

Miphkad Gate

Temple

East Gate

Mt. Moriah

Tyropoeon Valley

Royal Palace

Horse Gate

Kidron Valley

Olivet

Ophel

Valley Gate

Citadel

Water Gate

Mt. Zion

Spring Tower

N

W   E

S

Fountain Gate

Hinnom Valley

Scale of Feet

0   1000

Solomon's Temple

In what year of Solomon's reign did he begin to build the temple (1 Kings 6:1)? _____

How long did it take Solomon to build the temple (1 Kings 6:38)? _____

How long did it take Solomon to build his palace (1 Kings 7:1)? _____

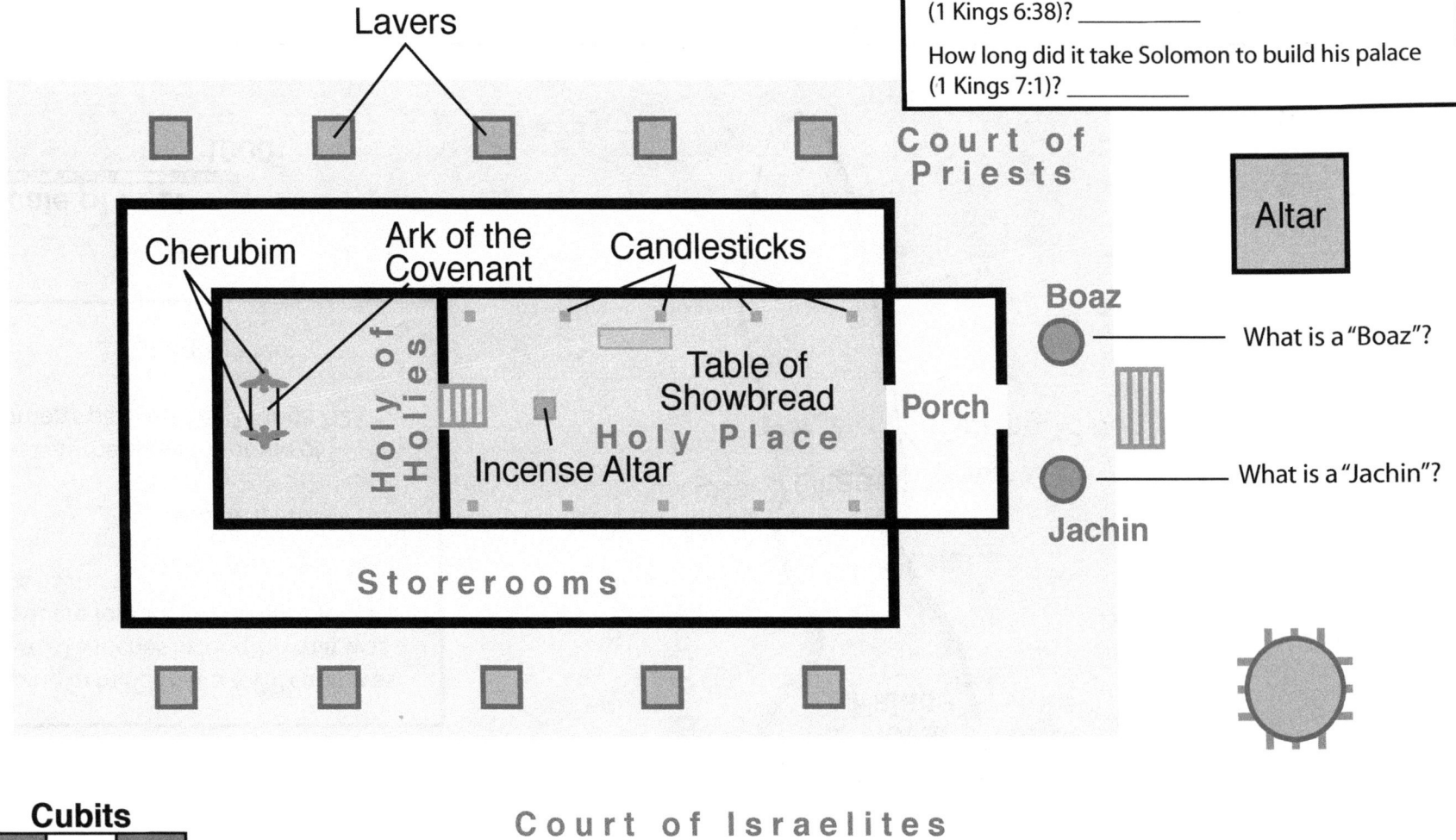

Lavers

Court of Priests

Altar

Cherubim

Ark of the Covenant

Candlesticks

Boaz

What is a "Boaz"?

Holy of Holies

Table of Showbread

Holy Place

Porch

Incense Altar

What is a "Jachin"?

Jachin

Storerooms

Cubits

0   30

Court of Israelites

What books of the Bible is Solomon credited with having written (either in part or whole)?
A. Psalms   B. Proverbs   C. Song of Solomon   D. Ecclesiastes

OLD TESTAMENT GEOGRAPHY
The Divided Kingdom – Part 1: Israel and Judah

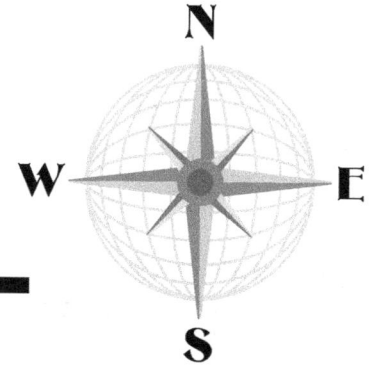

1. Where did the people of God gather to anoint Rehoboam (Solomon's son) as king? (1 Kings 12:1)
   A. Megiddo B. Shechem C. Shiloh D. Samaria E. Penuel

2. What request did God's people make of Rehoboam regarding taxation and service? (1 Kings 12:1-4)

   _____

   _____

3. Where had Jeroboam been living during Solomon's rule?
   A. Arabia B. Egypt C. Syria D. Babylon E. Chittim

4. Whose counsel did Rehoboam follow in deciding whether to lighten or increase the burden on Israel? What was his decision (1 Kings 12:6-15)?

   _____

   _____

5. What two things caused the division of the United Kingdom of Israel (1 Kings 11:4-13, 32, 36; 12:12-20)?

   _____

6. Which tribe(s) of Israel did NOT rebel against the rule of Rehoboam (1 Kings 12:20-24)?
   A. Judah B. Benjamin C. Simeon D. Dan E. Issachar

7. Where did the rebel king Jeroboam make his home (1 Kings 12:25)?
   A. Shechem B. Penuel C. Dan D. Bethel E. Jerusalem

8. Where did Jeroboam build two idols so the rebel tribes would not have to go to Jerusalem to worship (1 Kings 12:28-29)?
   A. Shechem B. Bethel C. Penuel D. Dan E. Shiloh

9. How many kings arose in the northern kingdom of Israel that were considered "good"?
   A. 0 B. 2 C. 5 D. 7 E. 11

10. Which city was the first capital of the northern kingdom of Israel (1 Kings 12:25; 15:33; 16:29)? Which was second? Which the third?
    A. Tirzah B. Shechem C. Bethel D. Megiddo E. Samaria

11. What city was the capital of the southern kingdom of Judah (1 Kings 14:21)?
    A. Tirzah B. Shechem C. Bethel D. Dor E. Jerusalem

KINGDOM

Divided Kingdom

☐ **Kingdom of Israel**

☐ **Kingdom of Judah**

c. 925 BC

What did Solomon do that caused the Lord to take the kingdom from him?

_____
_____
_____
_____
_____
_____

CAPTIAL CITIES
Judah's capital was Jerusalem.

Israel's capital was first Shechem, then Tirzah, and finally Samaria.

Circle the tribes below which comprised the northern kingdom. Put a box around those which comprised the southern kingdom.

Asher

Benjamin

Dan

Ephraim

Gad

Issachar

Judah

Levi

Manasseh

Naphtali

Reuben

Simeon

Zebulun

Tyre
PHOENICIA
Dan
ARAM
Ramah
Chinnereth
Hannathon
Aphek
Hammath
Dor
Megiddo
Ramoth-gilead
ISRAEL
Samaria ☆3 ☆2 Tirzah
Shechem ☆1
Penuel
Joppa
Shiloh
Jordan River
AMMON
Bethel
Rabbath
Gezer
Gibeon
Ashdod
Ekron ☆Jerusalem
Gath
Bethlehem
Ashkelon
JUDAH
Jahaz
Philistines
Gaza
Hebron
Salt Sea
En-gedi
Arad
MOAB
Hormah
Aroer
Kir-hareseth

Scale of Miles

0   50

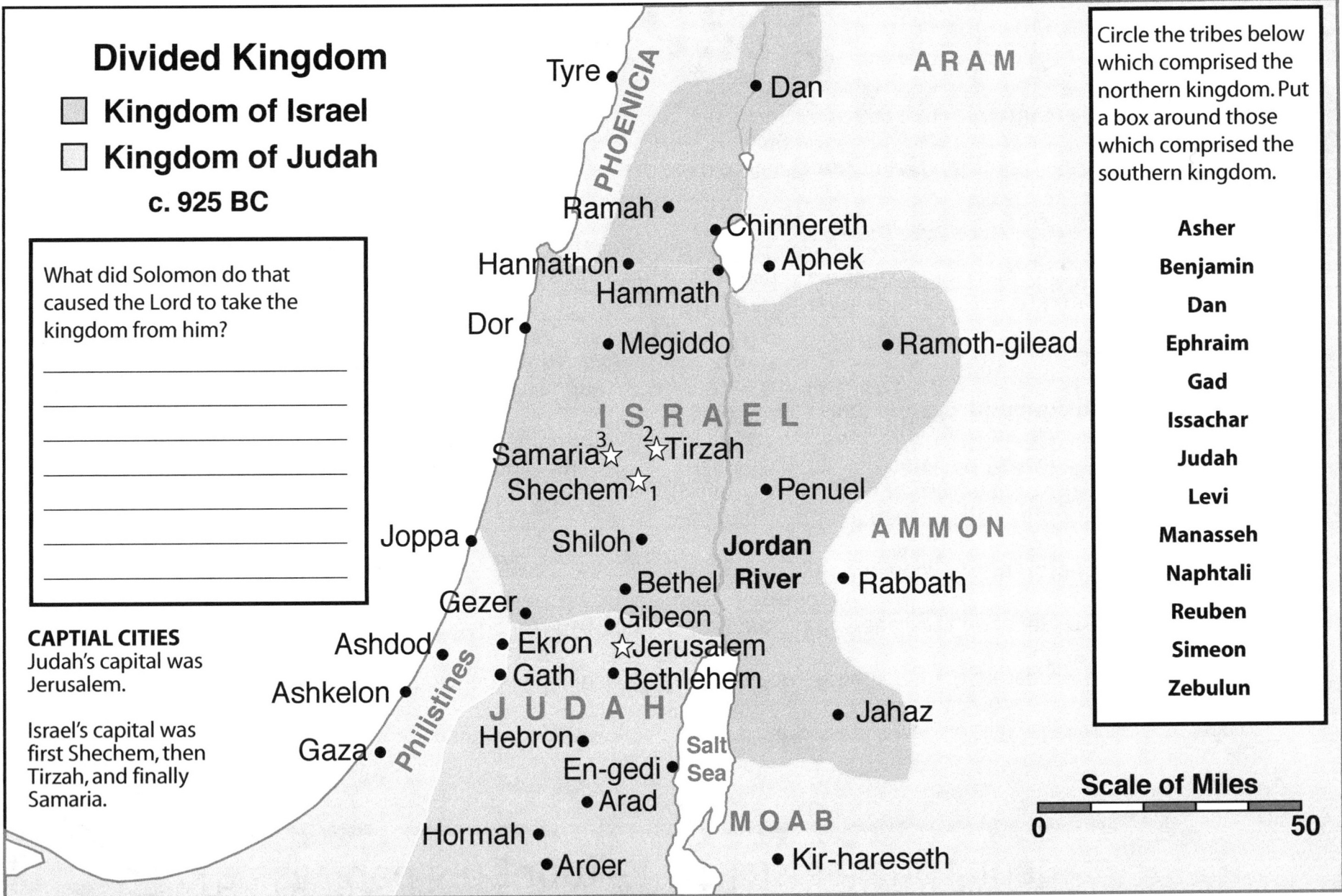

READ THE FOLLOWING TO HELP YOU WITH THE ANSWERS ABOVE

√ 1 Kings 11:1-43; 12:1-24

Question: Was it wrong for Israel to rebel against Rehoboam? ___ Yes ___ No Why? (See 2 Chron. 13:5-8.)

© 2020 Truth Publications, Inc.

OT Geography **38**

THE NATURE OF FALSE RELIGION

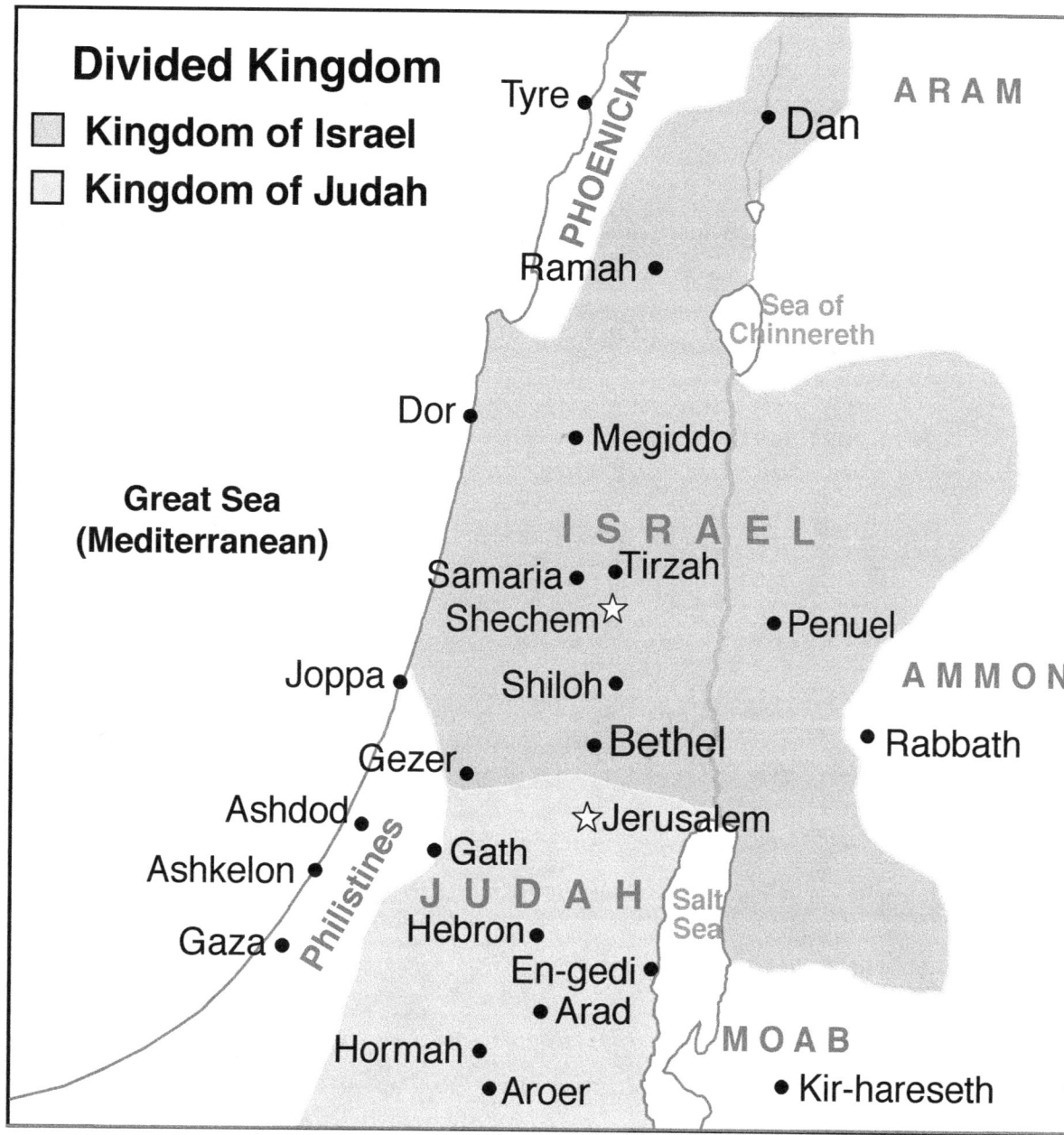

Divided Kingdom

☐ **Kingdom of Israel**

☐ **Kingdom of Judah**

Tyre

PHOENICIA

Dan

ARAM

Ramah

Sea of Chinnereth

Dor

Megiddo

Great Sea (Mediterranean)

ISRAEL

Samaria • Tirzah

Shechem ☆

Penuel

Joppa • Shiloh •

AMMON

Gezer • Bethel • Rabbath

Ashdod

☆ Jerusalem

Ashkelon • Gath

Philistines

JUDAH

Salt Sea

Gaza • Hebron •

En-gedi •

Arad •

Hormah •

MOAB

Aroer • Kir-hareseth

In 1 Kings 12:25-33 the Bible provides insight into how false religions get started. Read the passage and then answer the following:

1. Where did Jeroboam set up golden calves so the people could worship? (See vss. 28-29.)

_____

2. Circle the above two cities on the map. What do the two locations suggest?

_____

3. What was the source of Jeroboam's religion? (See vs. 33.)

_____

4. What was the motive behind Jeroboam's religion? (See vs. 26-27.)

_____

5. To what did Jeroboam appeal in order to get people to worship the calves? (See vs. 28.)

_____

6. In what way did Jeroboam's religion compare to true religion? (See vs. 32.)

_____

7. What prophecy was made against this false religion? (See 1 Kings 13:1-3; 2 Kings 23:16-17.)

_____

KINGS OF THE UNITED AND DIVIDED KINGDOM

The United Kingdom of Israel divided about 930 BC. The two kingdoms warred with each other and with other nations during this time. Then, about 200 years after the division, the northern kingdom was taken into Assyrian captivity. About 136 years later Judah was taken into Babylonian captivity.

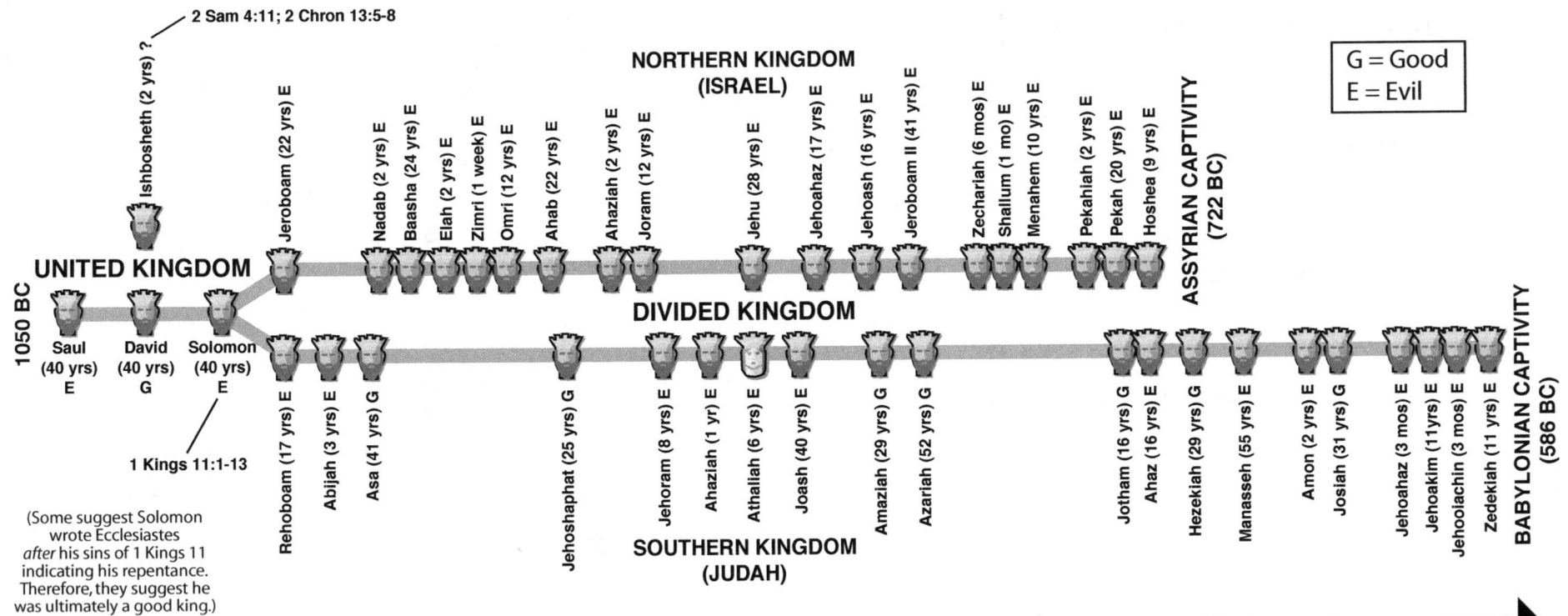

G = Good
E = Evil

2 Sam 4:11; 2 Chron 13:5-8

Ishbosheth (2 yrs) ?

NORTHERN KINGDOM (ISRAEL)

UNITED KINGDOM

1050 BC

Saul (40 yrs) E   David (40 yrs) G   Solomon (40 yrs) E

1 Kings 11:1-13

(Some suggest Solomon wrote Ecclesiastes *after* his sins of 1 Kings 11 indicating his repentance. Therefore, they suggest he was ultimately a good king.)

Jeroboam (22 yrs) E
Nadab (2 yrs) E
Baasha (24 yrs) E
Elah (2 yrs) E
Zimri (1 week) E
Omri (12 yrs) E
Ahab (22 yrs) E
Ahaziah (2 yrs) E
Joram (12 yrs) E
Jehu (28 yrs) E
Jehoahaz (17 yrs) E
Jehoash (16 yrs) E
Jeroboam II (41 yrs) E
Zechariah (6 mos) E
Shallum (1 mo) E
Menahem (10 yrs) E
Pekahiah (2 yrs) E
Pekah (20 yrs) E
Hoshea (9 yrs) E

ASSYRIAN CAPTIVITY (722 BC)

DIVIDED KINGDOM

BABYLONIAN CAPTIVITY (586 BC)

Rehoboam (17 yrs) E
Abijah (3 yrs) E
Asa (41 yrs) G
Jehoshaphat (25 yrs) G
Jehoram (8 yrs) E
Ahaziah (1 yr) E
Athaliah (6 yrs) E
Joash (40 yrs) E
Amaziah (29 yrs) G
Azariah (52 yrs) G
Jotham (16 yrs) G
Ahaz (16 yrs) E
Hezekiah (29 yrs) G
Manasseh (55 yrs) E
Amon (2 yrs) E
Josiah (31 yrs) G
Jehoahaz (3 mos) E
Jehoakim (11yrs) E
Jehoiachin (3 mos) E
Zedekiah (11 yrs) E

SOUTHERN KINGDOM (JUDAH)

Prophets of God bring warnings to Judah, Israel, and the surrounding nations of the dangers of disobedience.

QUESTIONS

1. Of the 39 kings that ruled in the two kingdoms, how many of them were murdered by the people they ruled? Make your guess below:

   A. 2   B. 5   C. 8   D. 11   E. 13

2. Where would we be able to read more about the kings except for the fact that the records have been lost (1 Kings 15:31; 1 Chron. 29:29)?

   _____

3. Were these lost records critical to our understanding of God and His dealings with His people? ___ Yes ___ No (See 2 Pet. 1:3.)

10 OLD TESTAMENT GEOGRAPHY
The Divided Kingdom – Part 2: The Prophets

1. Who was the prophet whose prayer for a drought resulted in no rain on the earth for 3 1/2 years (1 Kings 17:1; Jas. 5:17-18)?
   A. Elijah   B. Elisha   C. Ahijah   D. Shemaiah   E. Joel

2. Which prophet instructed Naaman, the captain of the armies of Syria to dip seven times in the Jordan to cure his leprosy (2 Kings 5:1-14)?
   A. Jonah   B. Elisha   C. Haggai   D. Micah   E. Joel

3. Which prophet went to preach to the Assyrians in Nineveh?
   A. Amos   B. Hosea   C. Joel   D. Jonah   E. Daniel

4. Amos compared evil Israel to what (Amos 8:1-2)?
   A. bad water   B. overripe fruit   C. a snake   D. a cistern

5. Which prophet to Judah prophesied about events that Peter said were fulfilled on the day of Pentecost (Acts 2:16-21)?
   A. Isaiah   B. Micah   C. Joel   D. Jonah   E. Ezekiel

6. Which prophet was instructed to marry a woman who would later commit adultery so he could compare his situation to that of Israel's spiritual adultery (Hos. 1:2)?
   A. Jeremiah   B. Obadiah   C. Malachi   D. Elisha   E. Hosea

7. Which prophet is perhaps best known for his Messianic prophesies—especially regarding the suffering Savior? (Isa. 53)
   A. Nahum   B. Elijah   C. Amos   D. Isaiah   E. Micah

8. This prophet preached repentance to Judah and spoke of Bethlehem as the birthplace of the Savior (Micah 5:2)?
   A. Joel   B. Micah   C. Isaiah   D. Amos   E. Jonah

9. Nahum warned this city, but they would not listen (Nahum 1:1).
   A. Tyre   B. Nineveh   C. Damascus   D. Babylon   E. Jerusalem

10. Zephaniah shows his royal ties by tracing his lineage back to what good king of Judah (Zeph. 1:1)?
    A. Hezekiah   B. Jotham   C. Amaziah   D. Jehoshaphat   E. Asa

11. This prophet is often referred to as the "weeping prophet."
    A. Isaiah   B. Joel   C. Nahum   D. Elisha   E. Jeremiah

12. This prophet tells Judah that their sins will cause them to be overtaken by the Chaldeans (Babylonians).
    A. Isaiah   B. Amos   C. Habakkuk   D. Nahum   E. Jonah

13. This prophet was about 17 years old when he was taken into Babylonian captivity. (Hint: The lions did not eat him!)
    A. Micah   B. Hosea   C. Malachi   D. Ezekiel   E. Daniel

14. What else was the prophet Ezekiel? (Ezek. 1:3; 3:17)
    A. A judge   B. A priest   C. A Levite   D. A watchman

15. Obadiah prophesied against what nation (Obad. 1:1-14)?
    A. Edom   B. Ammon   C. Syria   D. Babylon   E. Egypt

16. Upon their return from captivity, this prophet got mad at God's people because they were taking too long to restore the temple. (See Haggai 1:2-4.)
    A. Haggai   B. Zechariah   C. Obadiah   D. Malachi   E. Daniel

17. Upon their return from captivity, this prophet tried to encourage God's people to finish the temple.
    A. Malachi   B. Zechariah   C. Haggai   D. Ezekiel   E. Daniel

18. God was silent for 400 years following this prophet.
    A. Micah   B. Nahum   C. Malachi   D. Jonah   E. Amos

CHRONOLOGY OF PROPHETS AND TO WHOM THEY PROPHESIED

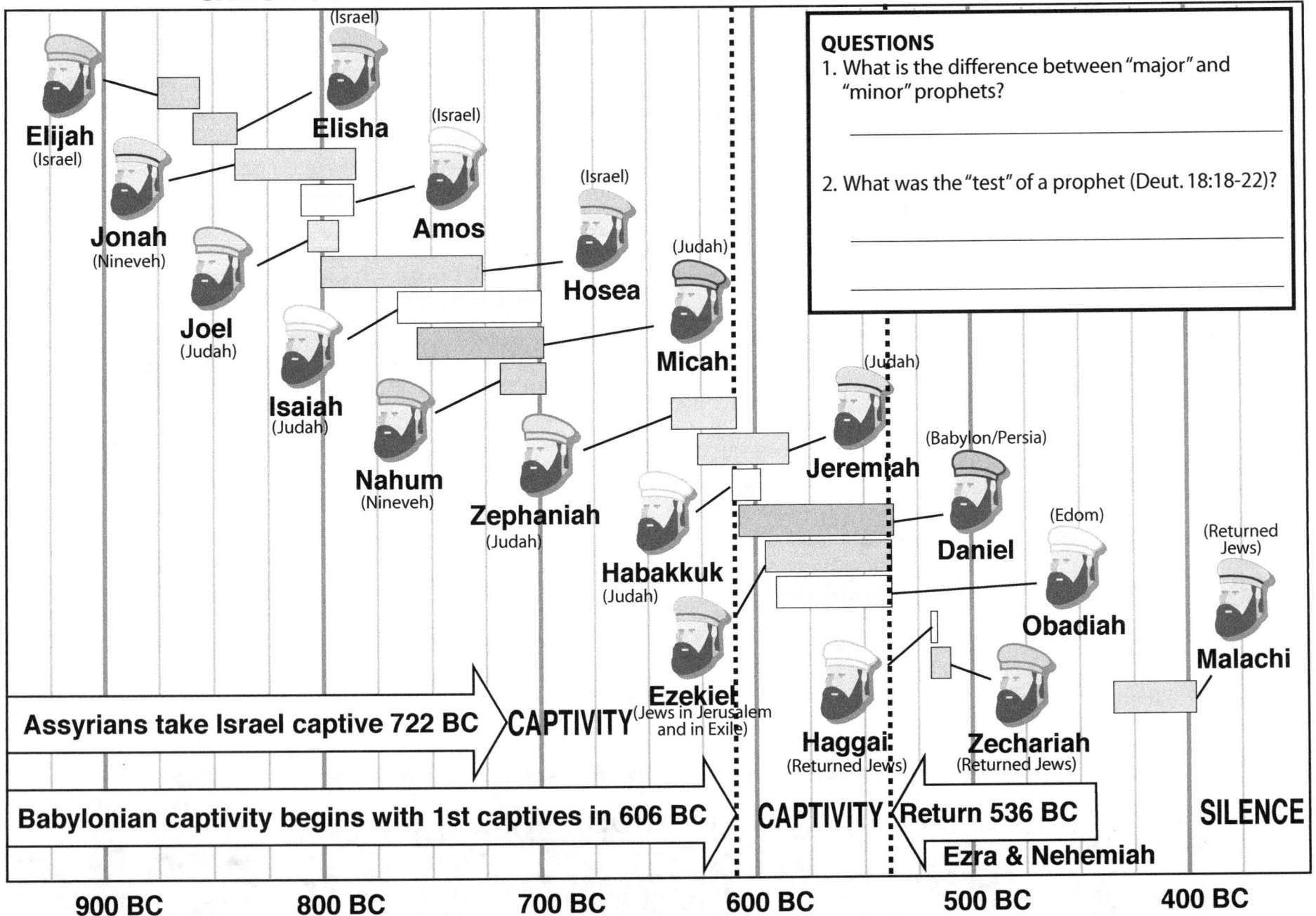

Elijah
(Israel)

(Israel)

Elisha

Jonah
(Nineveh)

(Israel)

Amos

(Israel)

Joel
(Judah)

Hosea

(Judah)

Isaiah
(Judah)

Micah

Nahum
(Nineveh)

Zephaniah
(Judah)

(Judah)

Jeremiah

(Babylon/Persia)

Habakkuk
(Judah)

Daniel

(Edom)

Obadiah

(Returned Jews)

Malachi

Ezekiel
(Jews in Jerusalem and in Exile)

Haggai
(Returned Jews)

Zechariah
(Returned Jews)

Assyrians take Israel captive 722 BC **CAPTIVITY**

Babylonian captivity begins with 1st captives in 606 BC **CAPTIVITY** **Return 536 BC** **SILENCE**

Ezra & Nehemiah

QUESTIONS
1. What is the difference between "major" and "minor" prophets?
_____
2. What was the "test" of a prophet (Deut. 18:18-22)?
_____

900 BC   800 BC   700 BC   600 BC   500 BC   400 BC

FAITH AND FLIGHT OF ELIJAH

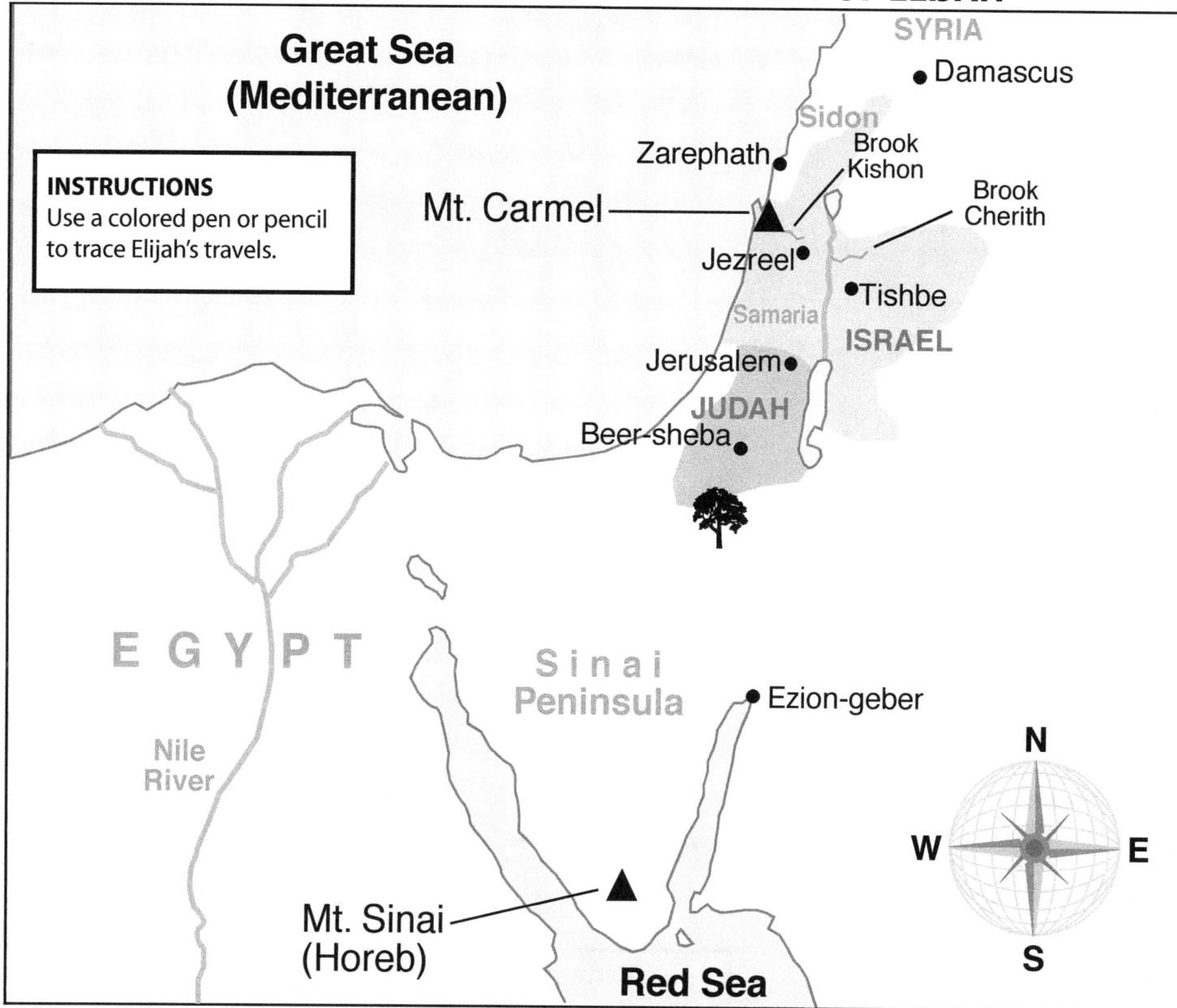

Great Sea (Mediterranean)

SYRIA

• Damascus

Sidon

Zarephath •

Brook Kishon

Brook Cherith

Mt. Carmel ▲

Jezreel •

• Tishbe

Samaria

ISRAEL

INSTRUCTIONS
Use a colored pen or pencil to trace Elijah's travels.

Jerusalem •

JUDAH

Beer-sheba •

E G Y P T

S i n a i Peninsula

• Ezion-geber

Nile River

N

W   E

S

Mt. Sinai (Horeb) ▲

Red Sea

1. Where was Elijah from?

2. Where did Elijah go to hide from Ahab?

3. Where did a widow provide for Elijah?

4. Where did the show-down between Elijah and the prophets of Baal occur?

5. Where did they kill the prophets of Baal?

6. Who threatened Elijah?

7. Where in Judah did Elijah flee?

8. To what mountain did Elijah flee?

9. What four men of the New Testament saw Elijah?

READ THE FOLLOWING TO HELP YOU WITH THE ANSWERS ABOVE
√ 1 Kings 17:1-24; 18:1-46; 19:1-18; Matthew 17:1-3

THE JOURNEY OF JONAH

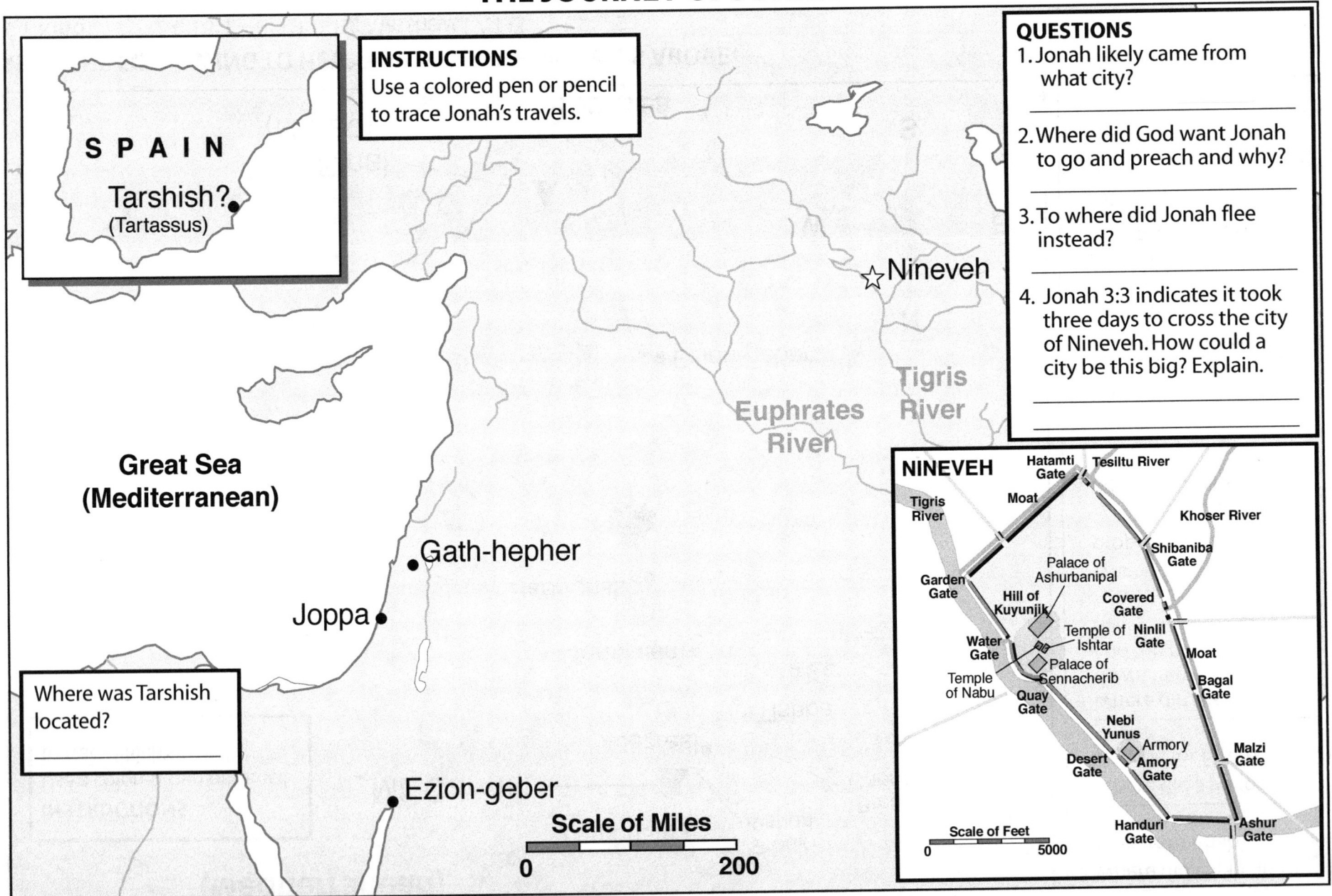

SPAIN

Tarshish?
(Tartassus)

INSTRUCTIONS
Use a colored pen or pencil to trace Jonah's travels.

QUESTIONS
1. Jonah likely came from what city?

_____

2. Where did God want Jonah to go and preach and why?

_____

3. To where did Jonah flee instead?

_____

4. Jonah 3:3 indicates it took three days to cross the city of Nineveh. How could a city be this big? Explain.

_____

☆ Nineveh

Tigris River

Euphrates River

Great Sea (Mediterranean)

Gath-hepher

Joppa

Where was Tarshish located?

_____

Ezion-geber

Scale of Miles

0   200

NINEVEH

Tigris River

Hatamti Gate

Tesiltu River

Moat

Khoser River

Shibaniba Gate

Garden Gate

Palace of Ashurbanipal

Hill of Kuyunjik

Covered Gate

Temple of Ishtar

Ninlil Gate

Water Gate

Palace of Sennacherib

Moat

Temple of Nabu

Quay Gate

Bagal Gate

Nebi Yunus

Armory

Malzi Gate

Desert Gate

Amory Gate

Scale of Feet

0   5000

Handuri Gate

Ashur Gate

READ THE FOLLOWING TO HELP YOU WITH THE ANSWERS ABOVE
√ Genesis 10:11-12; 2 Kings 14:25; 2 Chronicles 20:36; Jonah 1:1-3; 3:1-10; 4:11

OLD TESTAMENT GEOGRAPHY
The Fall and Captivity of Israel

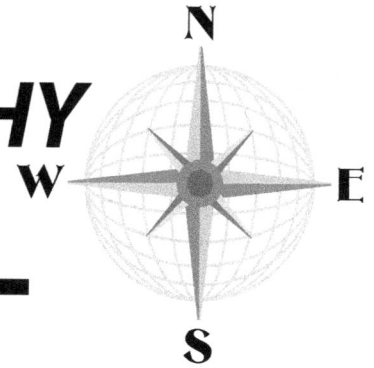

N W E S

1. Which empire defeated Israel and took the inhabitants captive (2 Kings 17:5-6)?
   A. Babylonian   B. Assyrian   C. Persian   D. Grecian   E. Roman

2. Who was the king of the empire above who first attacked Israel and forced them to pay tribute (2 Kings 15:29)?
   A. Pul   B. Tiglath-pileser   C. Sargon   D. Rezin   E. Shalmaneser

3. Which king of Israel rebelled against Assyria and formed a coalition with the king of Syria (2 Kings 16:5)?
   A. Pekah   B. Hoshea   C. Pekahiah   D. Menahem   E. Shallum

4. The newly formed coalition between Israel and Syria tried to force what king of Judah into the coalition (2 Kings 16:5)?
   A. Hezekiah   B. Manasseh   C. Jotham   D. Ahaz   E. Azariah

5. What "deal" did the king of Judah make with the Assyrian king (2 Kings 16:7-9)? Was the deal a good one (2 Chron. 28:19-21)?

   _____

   _____

6. In what city was Rezin, the king of Syria, killed (2 Kings 16:9)?
   A. Jerusalem   B. Bethel   C. Damascus   D. Hazor   E. Megiddo

7. Who was the final king of Israel (2 Kings 17:1-2)?
   A. Hoshea   B. Pekahiah   C. Menahem   D. Jehu   E. Ahab

8. With the king of what country did Israel's last king attempt to form an alliance against the Assyrians (2 Kings 17:3-4)?
   A. Syria   B. Arabia   C. Phoenicia   D. Edom   E. Egypt

9. What was the capital city of the northern kingdom during its final days? (2 Kings 17:5)
   A. Shiloh   B. Samaria   C. Megiddo   D. Bethel   E. Tirzah

10. How many years was the capital city of Israel besieged before it finally fell (2 Kings 17:5)?
    A. 1 year   B. 2 years   C. 3 years   D. 4 years   E. 5 years

11. Where *specifically* did the Assyrians take the people of Israel (2 Kings 17:6)? Find and circle the area on the map on page 47.

    _____

    _____

12. When the Assyrians carried away conquered people into captivity, they resettled other captives in the land that had been vacated. The few remaining poor Jews of Israel intermarried with the arriving foreign captives. What mixed race did these people become who were later despised by the Jews during New Testament times?
    A. Syrians   B. Samaritans   C. Edomites   D. Ammonites

THE ATTACK OF THE ASSYRIANS

Kingdom of Israel
Kingdom of Judah

1. Tiglath-pileser (Pul) brings his forces westward forcing Syria, Phoenicia, Israel and Arabia to pay tribute.

2. Pekah, king of Israel, forms coalition with the king of Syria, to fend off Assyrian forces. They attempt to force Judah into the alliance by attacking Jerusalem.

3. Ahaz, king of Judah, sends treasures from the house of God to Tiglath-pileser asking him for help against the coalition.

4. Assyrian troops advance, conquering Philistia and proceeding into Egypt.

5. After a three year siege, the capital city of Samaria falls in 722 BC. Israel is taken captive and other foreign captives are brought in to inhabit the land.

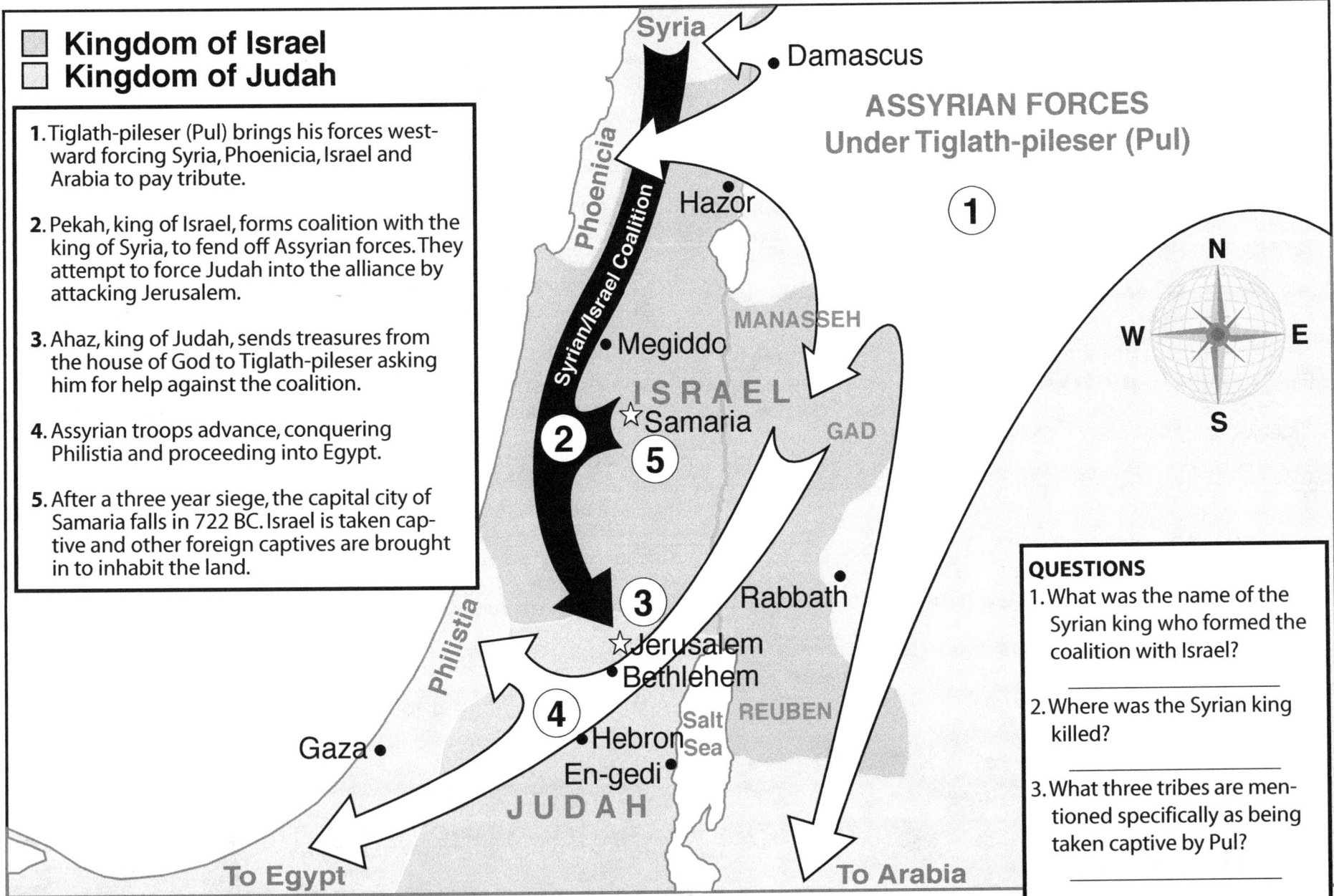

Syria

Damascus

ASSYRIAN FORCES
Under Tiglath-pileser (Pul)

Phoenicia

Hazor

Syrian/Israel Coalition

MANASSEH

Megiddo

ISRAEL

Samaria

GAD

Rabbath

Jerusalem
Bethlehem

REUBEN

Salt Sea

Philistia

Gaza

Hebron

En-gedi

JUDAH

To Egypt

To Arabia

N / W / E / S

QUESTIONS

1. What was the name of the Syrian king who formed the coalition with Israel?
   _____

2. Where was the Syrian king killed?
   _____

3. What three tribes are mentioned specifically as being taken captive by Pul?
   _____
   _____
   _____

READ THE FOLLOWING TO HELP YOU WITH THE ANSWERS ABOVE
√ 2 Kings 15:29, 32, 37; 16:5-9; 17:1-6; 1 Chronicles 5:26

THE FALL AND CAPTIVITY OF ISRAEL

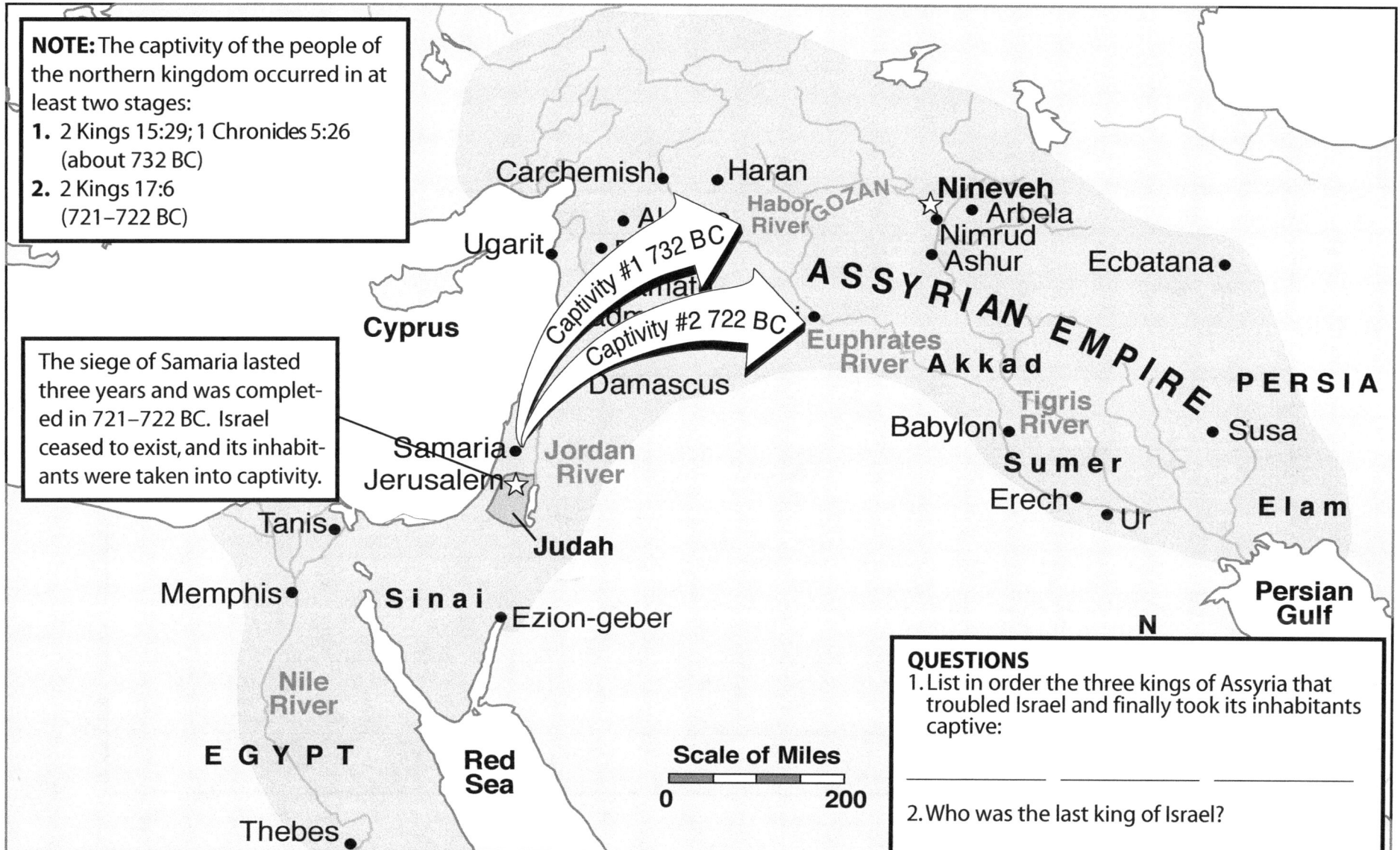

NOTE: The captivity of the people of the northern kingdom occurred in at least two stages:

1. 2 Kings 15:29; 1 Chronides 5:26 (about 732 BC)
2. 2 Kings 17:6 (721–722 BC)

The siege of Samaria lasted three years and was completed in 721–722 BC. Israel ceased to exist, and its inhabitants were taken into captivity.

Carchemish · Haran

Habor GOZAN
River

Nineveh ☆ · Arbela
Nimrud
Ashur · Ecbatana ·

A S S Y R I A N E M P I R E

Ugarit ·

Captivity #1 732 BC

Captivity #2 722 BC

Cyprus

Euphrates River **Akkad**

P E R S I A

Damascus

Tigris River

Babylon · · Susa

S u m e r

Samaria · Jordan River

Erech · · Ur

E l a m

Jerusalem ☆

Judah

Tanis ·

Memphis ·

S i n a i

· Ezion-geber

Persian Gulf

N

Nile River

E G Y P T

Red Sea

Scale of Miles

0   200

Thebes ·

QUESTIONS

1. List in order the three kings of Assyria that troubled Israel and finally took its inhabitants captive:

_____ _____ _____

2. Who was the last king of Israel?

_____

3. From whom did the last king of Israel attempt to get help against the Assyrians?

_____

READ THE FOLLOWING TO HELP YOU WITH THE ANSWERS ABOVE

√ 2 Kings 15:19, 29; 17:1-6; Isaiah 20:1

THE CAUSE OF ISRAEL'S FALL AND CAPTIVITY

INSTRUCTIONS: Read 2 Kings 17:7-18 and list below all the reasons God allowed the destruction of Israel by the Assyrians. What lessons can we glean from the story of Israel's fall and captivity?

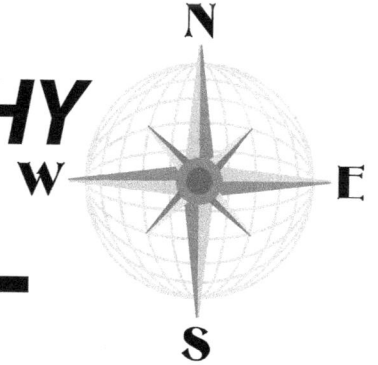

1. What good king replaced Ahaz in Judah (2 Chron. 29:1)?
   A. Jotham   B. Hezekiah   C. Manasseh   D. Joash   E. Hoshea

2. What good things did Ahaz's replacement do (2 Chron. 29:3,5,15, 18-19, 21f)?
   A. Repaired the doors of the house of the Lord
   B. Sanctified the house of the Lord
   C. Cleansed the house of the Lord
   D. Prepared and sanctified the vessels of the house of the Lord
   E. Made sacrificial offerings to the Lord

3. King Hezekiah sent out letters to the remnant of Jews living in Israel encouraging them to come worship in Jerusalem. Many scoffed at the suggestion. However, some did come from what tribes (2 Chron. 30:5-11, 18)?
   A. Ephraim   B. Asher   C. Manasseh   D. Issachar   E. Zebulun

4. In what year of Hezekiah's reign did Assyria under Sennacherib attempt to defeat Jerusalem and take its inhabitants captive (2 Kings 18:13)?
   A. 5   B. 11   C. 14   D. 17   E. 21   D. 23

5. Who became king *after* Hezekiah? Was he good or bad?
   A. Manasseh   B. Ahaz   C. Jotham   D. Azariah   E. Joash

6. In what valley did the wicked king above sacrifice his sons (2 Chron. 33:6)?
   A. Kidron   B. Hinnom   C. Doves   D. Jezreel   E. Iphtahel

7. What two nations joined forces to defeat the Assyrians in about 612 BC?
   A. Babylonians   B. Grecians   C. Romans   D. Egyptians   E. Medes

8. What king of Babylon took treasure and captives from Judah in about 606 BC—the first captivity (Dan. 1:1-6)?
   A. Nod   B. Nebuchadnezzar   C. Nabopolassar   D. Necho

9. What advice did Jeremiah the prophet give to the people regarding the second Babylonian captivity about to occur (Jer. 25:1-14; 27:17-18)? How long did he say it would last?

   _____

   _____

   _____

ASSYRIANS PUT DOWN REBELLION

Scale of Miles

0   50

Sennacherib's forces destroy Tyre and then move south and destroy Joppa. An Egyptian army is defeated further south. Then Sennacherib's forces attack Judah's fortified cities including Bethel and encircle Jerusalem.

QUESTIONS

1. What did Hezekiah build to improve Jerusalem's ability to survive Assyrian attack?

_____

2. Where did Hezekiah send messengers to Sennacherib promising to pay tribute?

_____

3. The Assyrians were asked to speak in what language so the soldiers on the walls of Jerusalem would not understand?

_____

4. What prophet of God promised deliverance of Hezekiah and the people?

_____

5. What happened to the Assyrian army and later to Sennacherib?

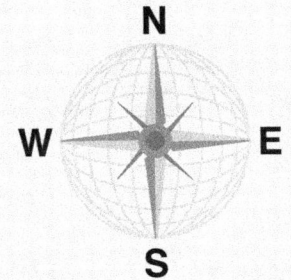

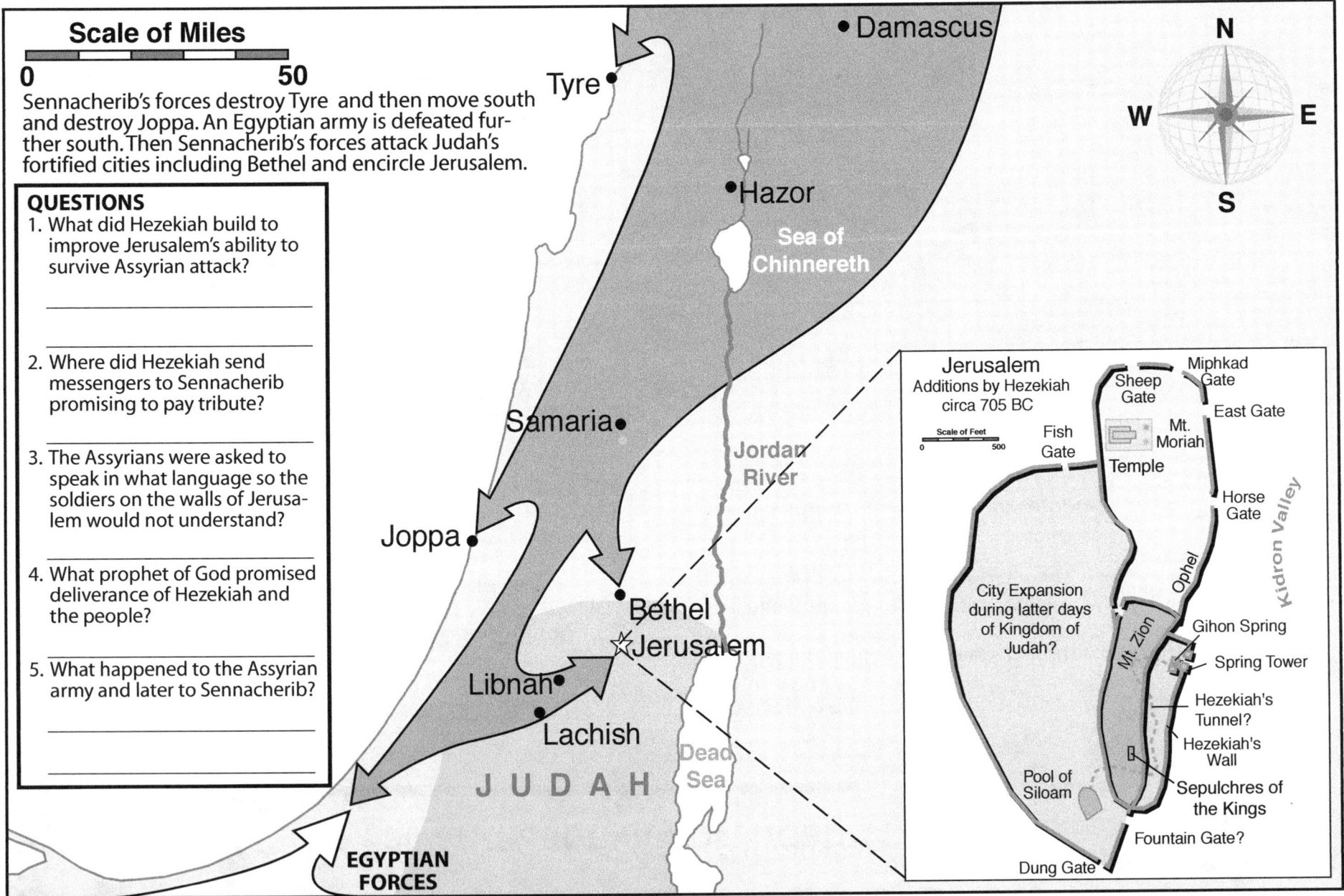

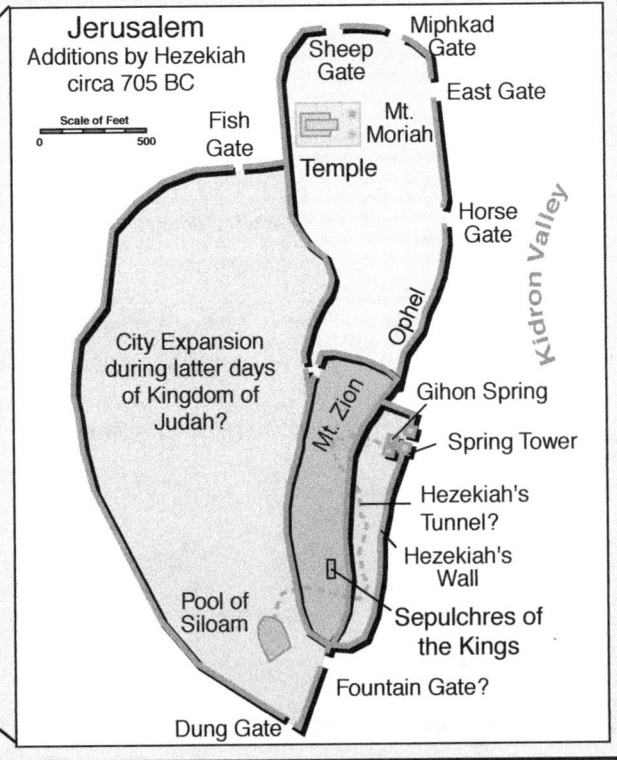

_____

Damascus

Tyre

Hazor

Sea of Chinnereth

Samaria

Jordan River

Joppa

Bethel
☆ Jerusalem

Libnah

Lachish

Dead Sea

J U D A H

EGYPTIAN FORCES

N
W   E
S

Jerusalem
Additions by Hezekiah circa 705 BC

Scale of Feet

0   500

Sheep Gate

Miphkad Gate

Fish Gate

Mt. Moriah

East Gate

Temple

Horse Gate

Ophel

Kidron Valley

City Expansion during latter days of Kingdom of Judah?

Mt. Zion

Gihon Spring

Spring Tower

Hezekiah's Tunnel?

Hezekiah's Wall

Pool of Siloam

Sepulchres of the Kings

Fountain Gate?

Dung Gate

READ THE FOLLOWING TO HELP YOU WITH THE ANSWERS ABOVE

√ 2 Chronicles 32:5, 30; 2 Kings 18:9-37; 19:1-37; Isaiah 37:33-35

THE FALL OF ASSYRIA – 612 BC

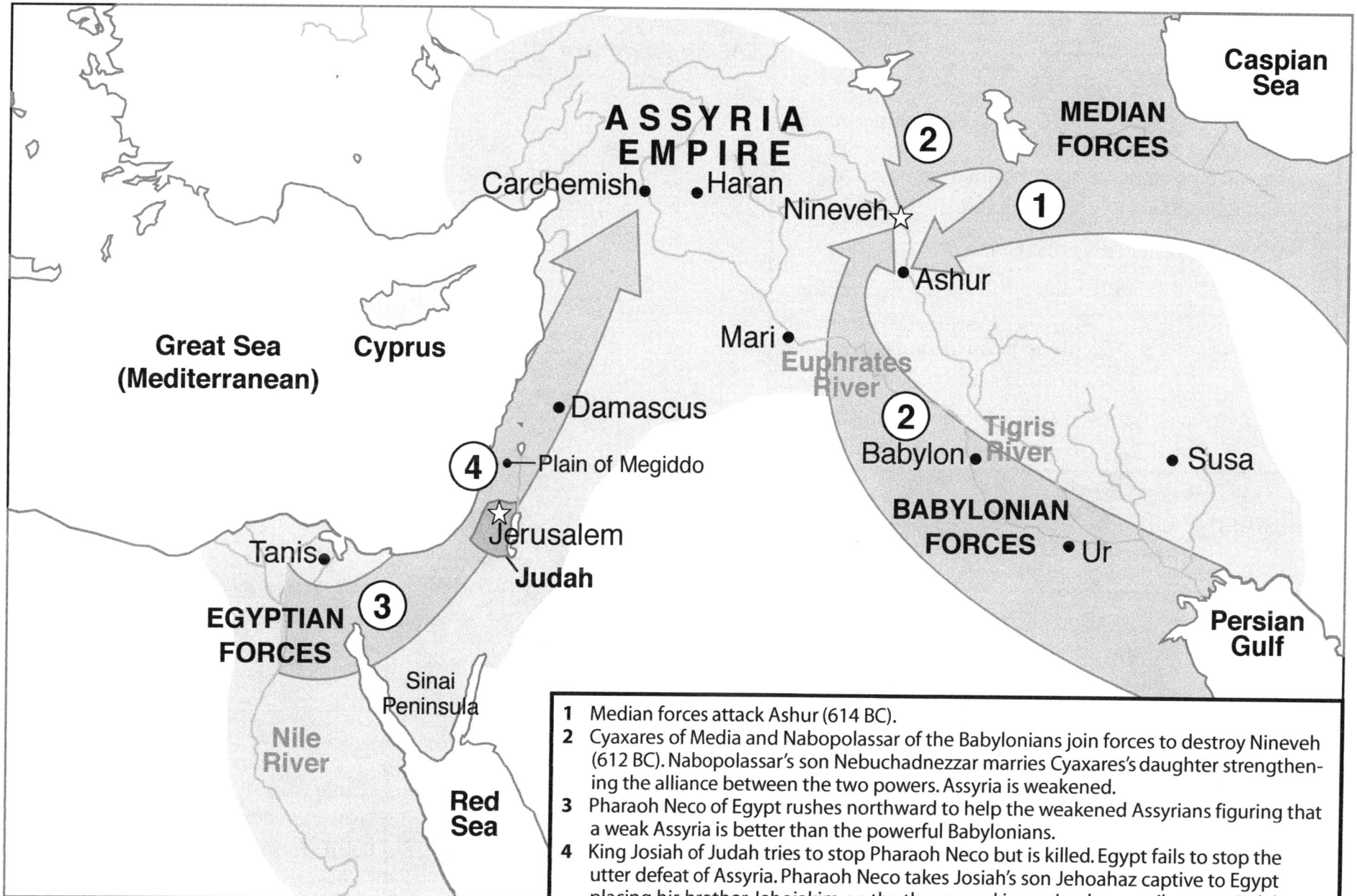

Caspian Sea

MEDIAN FORCES

ASSYRIA EMPIRE

Carchemish• •Haran

② ①

Nineveh ☆

•Ashur

Great Sea (Mediterranean)

Cyprus

Mari•

Euphrates River

•Damascus

Tigris River

②

Babylon• •Susa

④ •Plain of Megiddo

BABYLONIAN FORCES

☆ Jerusalem

•Ur

Tanis•

Judah

③

EGYPTIAN FORCES

Sinai Peninsula

Persian Gulf

Nile River

Red Sea

1 Median forces attack Ashur (614 BC).
2 Cyaxares of Media and Nabopolassar of the Babylonians join forces to destroy Nineveh (612 BC). Nabopolassar's son Nebuchadnezzar marries Cyaxares's daughter strengthening the alliance between the two powers. Assyria is weakened.
3 Pharaoh Neco of Egypt rushes northward to help the weakened Assyrians figuring that a weak Assyria is better than the powerful Babylonians.
4 King Josiah of Judah tries to stop Pharaoh Neco but is killed. Egypt fails to stop the utter defeat of Assyria. Pharaoh Neco takes Josiah's son Jehoahaz captive to Egypt placing his brother Jehoiakim on the throne and imposing heavy tribute on Judah (2 Chron. 35:20-27; 36:1-4). Meanwhile, the Medes take the land to the north and northwest while Babylonia turns its attention to Egypt and Canaan to the west.

BABYLON TAKES JUDAH CAPTIVE

Captivity #1 – Nobility taken captive including Daniel and his three friends (2 Kings 20:14-19; Dan. 1:1-6)

Captivity #2 – Jehoiachin and 10,000 taken into captivity (2 Kings 24:8-15)

Captivity #3 – Zedekiah taken and the destruction of the temple and walls of Jerusalem (2 Kings 25:1-15)

Caspian Sea

Carchemish • Haran •

Nineveh •

MEDIAN EMPIRE

BABYLONIAN EMPIRE

Ashur •

Great Sea (Mediterranean)

Cyprus

Damas...

Mari •

Euphrates River

Captivity #1 606 BC

Captivity #2 596 BC

Captivity #3 586 BC

Babylon ☆ Tigris River

• Susa

Jerusalem •

Tanis •

Judah

EGYPT

Sinai Peninsula

Nile River

Red Sea

QUESTIONS

1. What king of Judah became servant to Nebuchadnezzar for three years? _____

2. What well-known prophet was carried away in the first Babylonian captivity?_____
   About how old is it estimated he was? _____

3. Nebuchadnezzar installed the last king of Judah. What was his name? _____

4. What did Nebuchadnezzar do when the king he had installed rebelled? What did he do to the king's sons? What did he do to the king?
   _____
   _____
   _____

READ THE FOLLOWING TO HELP YOU WITH THE ANSWERS ABOVE
√ 2 Kings 20:14-19; 24:1-20; 25:1-12; 2 Chronicles 36:9-21; Ezekiel 17:15-20

LESSON 13 — OLD TESTAMENT GEOGRAPHY
Captivity and Return

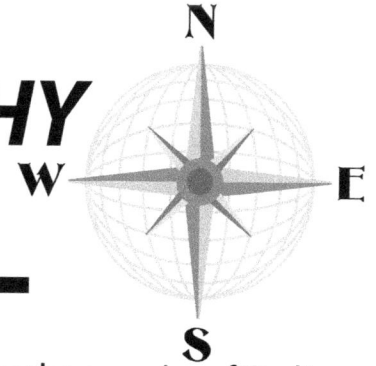

1. Did God fulfill His promise to Abraham to make of his offspring a great nation and to give them land for an inheritance? (See Josh. 21:43-45.) ___ Yes ___ No

2. What prophetic promise is made by God to His people who are far from home in captivity? (Deut. 30:1-6; Ezek. 11:13, 16-21)
   _____
   _____

3. Look back at page 42 and indicate below when Isaiah lived and prophesied:
   _____

4. Read Isaiah 44:24-28; 45:1-7. Name the king God indicated would restore Jerusalem and the temple.
   _____

5. What orders did Cyrus the king of Persia give regarding the house of the Lord in Jerusalem (Ezra 1:1-4)?
   _____
   _____

6. The Lord stirred the people of what tribe(s) to go and rebuild the temple (Ezra 1:5)?
   A. Judah   B. Issachar   C. Benjamin   D. Asher   E. Levi

7. Who led the first group of homebound Jews (Ezra 2:2)?
   A. Ezra   B. Nehemiah   C. Zerubbabel   D. Daniel   E. Mordecai

8. What was the total number of people making preparation to go back to Jerusalem and rebuild the temple (Ezra 2:64)?
   _____

9. Work on the temple stopped because the enemies of God's people sent a message to King Cyrus's successor telling him what about the Jews (Ezra 4:13-21)?
   _____
   _____

10. Who came to power and allowed work on the temple to resume (Ezra 4:24)?
    A. Darius the Mede   B. Cyrus   C. Darius of Persia   D. Artaxerxes

11. What king came to power who later made Esther queen and nearly destroyed all the Jews ? (Esth. 1:1)
    A. Darius   B. Cyrus   C. Xerxes   D. Artaxerxes   E. Ahasuerus

12. King Artaxerxes allowed what priest to lead a second group of about 2,000 Jews back to Jerusalem (Ezra 7:1,6, 11-13)?
    A. Ezra   B. Nehemiah   C. Zerubbabel   D. Daniel   E. Mordecai

13. What cupbearer to King Artaxerxes led a third group of Jews back to Jerusalem to rebuild its walls (Neh. 2:1-8)?
    A. Ezra   B. Nehemiah   C. Zerubbabel   D. Daniel   E. Mordecai

14. How long did it take to complete the walls (Neh. 6:15-16)?
    A. 52 days   B. 62 days   C. 72 days   D. 82 days   E. 92 days

15. Nehemiah went back to Susa for awhile. What did he find when he later returned to Jerusalem (Neh. 13:23-29)?
    _____
    _____

16. What problems did Malachi describe about the worship of the people and what prophecy did he make for the future (Mal. 1:7-13; 3:1-4)? _____
    _____

THE RISE OF THE MEDO-PERSIAN EMPIRE UNDER CYRUS

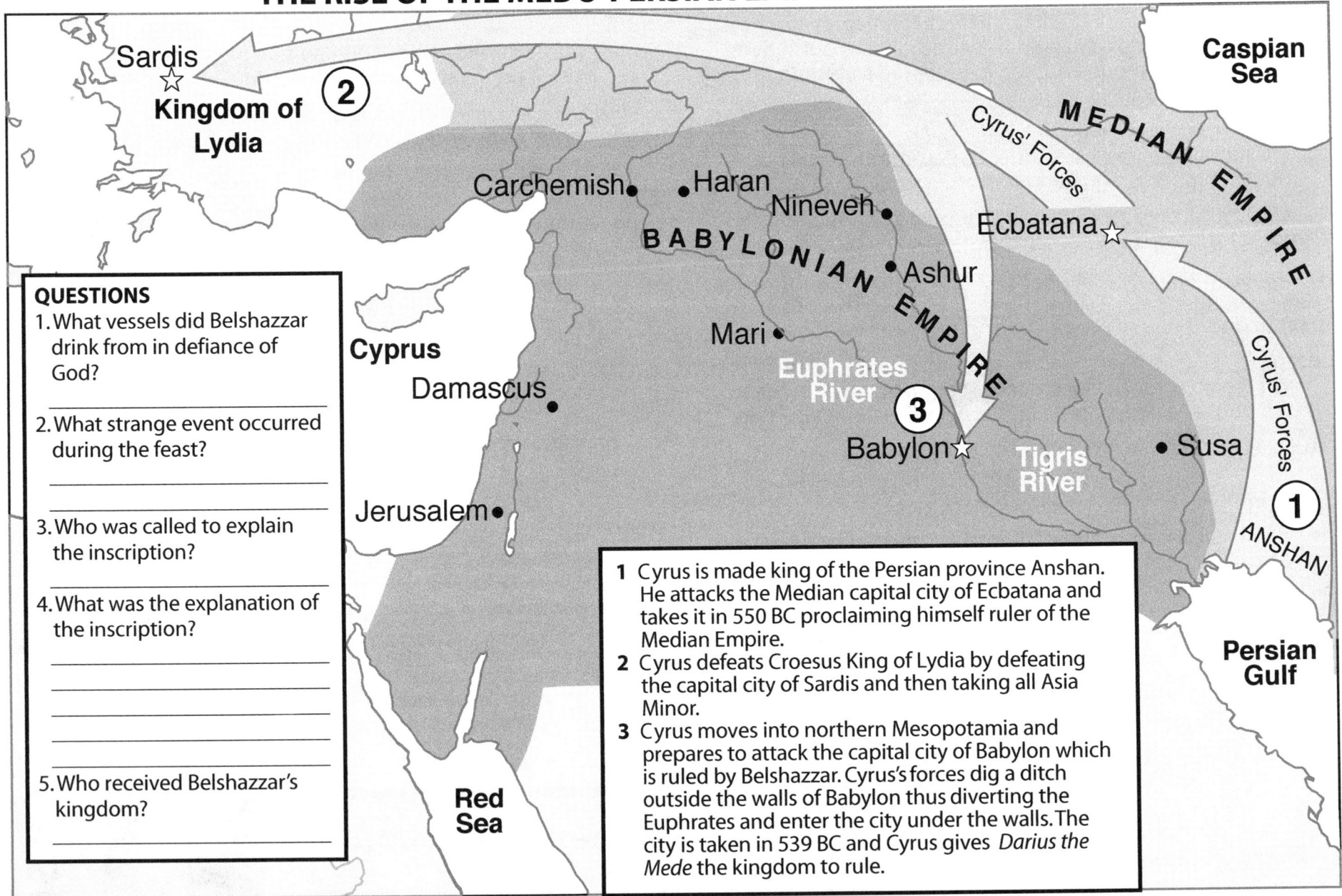

Caspian Sea

Sardis

Kingdom of Lydia ②

MEDIAN EMPIRE

Cyrus' Forces

Carchemish · Haran

Nineveh ·

Ecbatana ☆

BABYLONIAN EMPIRE

· Ashur

Cyprus

Mari ·

Euphrates River ③

Cyrus' Forces

Damascus ·

Babylon ☆

Tigris River

· Susa

Jerusalem ·

ANSHAN ①

Persian Gulf

QUESTIONS

1. What vessels did Belshazzar drink from in defiance of God?
   _____
   _____

2. What strange event occurred during the feast?
   _____
   _____
   _____

3. Who was called to explain the inscription?
   _____
   _____

4. What was the explanation of the inscription?
   _____
   _____
   _____
   _____

5. Who received Belshazzar's kingdom?
   _____
   _____

1 Cyrus is made king of the Persian province Anshan. He attacks the Median capital city of Ecbatana and takes it in 550 BC proclaiming himself ruler of the Median Empire.

2 Cyrus defeats Croesus King of Lydia by defeating the capital city of Sardis and then taking all Asia Minor.

3 Cyrus moves into northern Mesopotamia and prepares to attack the capital city of Babylon which is ruled by Belshazzar. Cyrus's forces dig a ditch outside the walls of Babylon thus diverting the Euphrates and enter the city under the walls. The city is taken in 539 BC and Cyrus gives *Darius the Mede* the kingdom to rule.

Red Sea

READ THE FOLLOWING TO HELP YOU WITH THE ANSWERS ABOVE

√ Daniel 5

HOME AGAIN HEROES

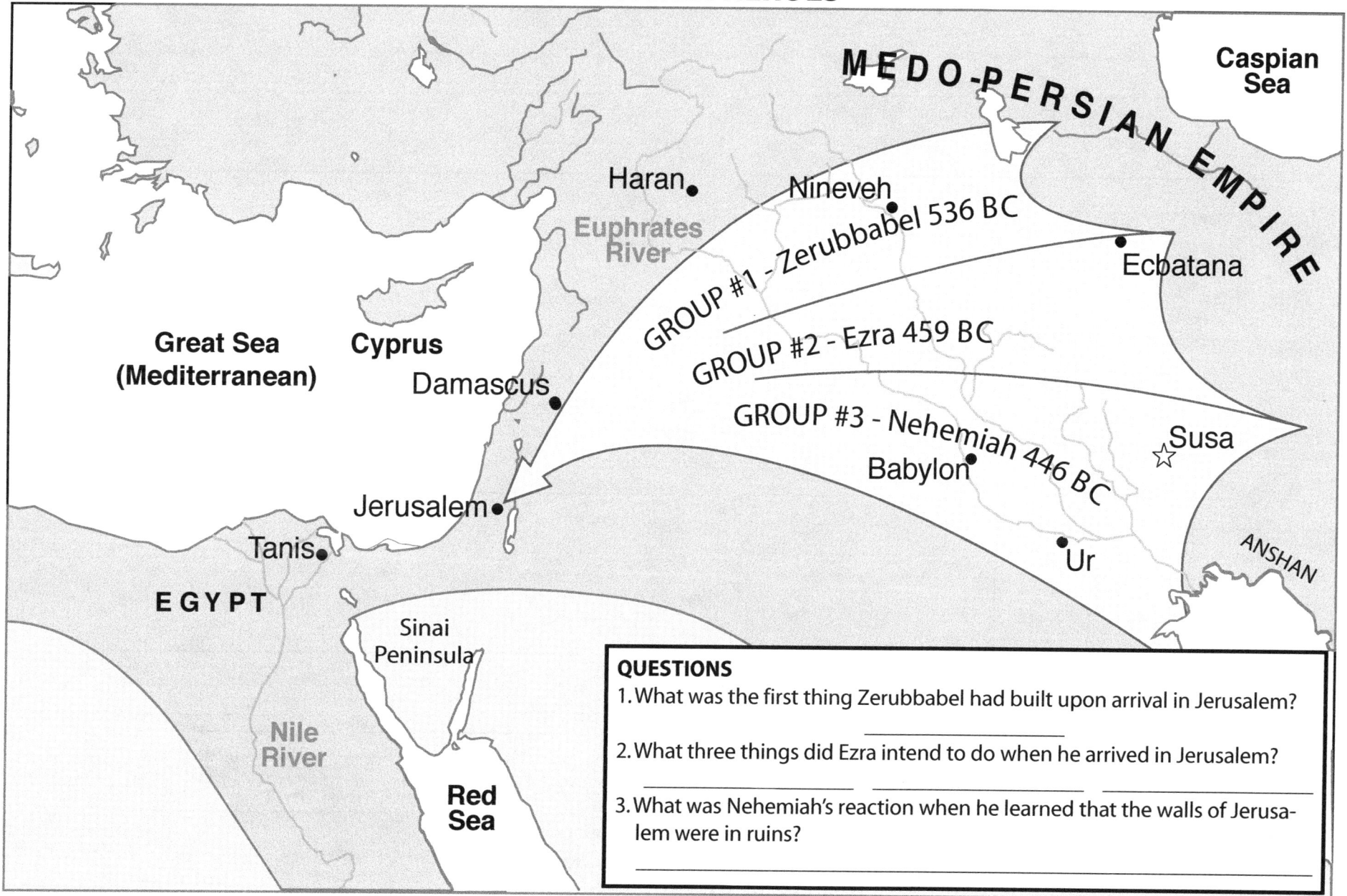

Caspian Sea

MEDO-PERSIAN EMPIRE

Haran

Nineveh

Euphrates River

GROUP #1 - Zerubbabel 536 BC

Ecbatana

Great Sea (Mediterranean)

Cyprus

Damascus

GROUP #2 - Ezra 459 BC

GROUP #3 - Nehemiah 446 BC

Susa

Jerusalem

Babylon

Tanis

Ur

EGYPT

ANSHAN

Sinai Peninsula

Nile River

Red Sea

QUESTIONS

1. What was the first thing Zerubbabel had built upon arrival in Jerusalem?
   _____

2. What three things did Ezra intend to do when he arrived in Jerusalem?
   _____ _____ _____

3. What was Nehemiah's reaction when he learned that the walls of Jerusa-lem were in ruins?
   _____

READ THE FOLLOWING TO HELP YOU WITH THE ANSWERS ABOVE
√ Ezra 3:1-2; 7:6-10; Nehemiah 1:1-9

FINAL QUIZ

Teacher: Use this page to pose questions to your class regarding the material covered during the quarter.

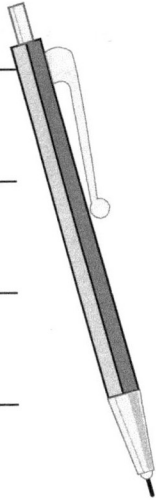

1. _____

2. _____

3. _____

4. _____

5. _____

6. _____

7. _____

8. _____

9. _____

10. _____

11. _____

12. _____

13. _____

14. _____

15. _____

16. _____

17. _____

18. _____

19. _____

20. _____